THE ART OF STANDING STILL

When Still Doesn't Mean Stuck

THE ART OF STANDING STILL

When Still Doesn't Mean Stuck

by Patricia Walden

Published by
GYT World

The Art of Standing Still… When Still Doesn't Mean Stuck
Published by: GYT World
www.theartofstandingstill.com

This book or parts thereof may not be reproduced in any form, stored in a retrieval system, or transmitted in any form by any means—electronic, mechanical, photocopy, recording, or otherwise—without prior written permission of the publisher, except as provided by United States copyright law. For information, contact, GYT World, www.theartofstandingstill.com

All scripture reference and quotations, unless otherwise indicated, are taken from the King James Version of the Holy Bible.

 Copyright ©2010, by Patricia Walden, GYT World
ALL RIGHTS RESERVED

How to Order:
Additional copies of this book can be purchased through GYT World. Contact us for more information by:

Email: info@theartofstandingstill.com

ISBN-13: 978-1--61623-962-6

Cover design by Dana Taylor

Printed in the United States of America

To the Reader

For all those who have been in a certain place of unrest, I am hopeful that you will find – if not relief – at least comfort in knowing that while you might be lonely, you are never alone. And that our still-ability in our time of testing will not only allow us to test the times we are able to stand, but to also stand the tests of time.

....

Your comments are welcome. To comment on any parts of this book, please send emails to info@theartofstandingstill.com or artofstandingstill@yahoo.com.

The Art of Standing Still...
When Still Doesn't Mean Stuck

Table of Contents

Introduction
1

Chapter One
Taking a Stand
7

Chapter Two
Night Blindness
21

Chapter Three
The Dance of Night Stillness
39

Chapter Four
Seek and Go Hide
51

Chapter Five
Mobile Mayhem
57

Chapter Six
The Breaking of Day
63

Chapter Seven
The Stillness that Moves Me
69

Chapter Eight
A Season of Stillness
83

Chapter Nine
Stillness on Demand
87

Chapter Ten
At the Center of your Stillness
91

Contents' Summary:
Take a stand to come out of night blindness so that you can dance the dance of night stillness, which will bring you to the point of seeking to go hide in Christ after coming up out of mobile mayhem and experiencing the breaking of day. Stillness will move you into a season of stillness on demand and bring you to a place where you can find sweet rest at the center of your stillness. So don't be stuck. Just be still.

Acknowledgement

Thanks be to God for the promise that has been fulfilled in my life. I am forever grateful and still-fully committed to the command of God's voice and the leading of His hand. I am extremely grateful to Veleta Jackson, my mother, who is responsible for my spiritual posture and my straight and narrow upbringing. Did I say straight?

I am sure there was a time in my mother's life - with all of the responsibilities she had - when she wishes she could have been still; but all of her responsibilities kept her moving. Nonetheless, I am most appreciative for the sacrifices that she made for me and my siblings – Winston, Carlos, Keith and Sharon. She did without, so that we could have what we needed. I know that had she not sacrificed her desires, our needs may not necessarily have been met. So, thank you mother, for your exemplary life. I love you always.

....

Introduction

There seems to be some sort of fallacy to the truth about progression. Firstly, who does not want to move forward? The false truth is that to progress, you have to be moving. I have reached a point in my life, where I have to move forwardly – hence this particular writing. However, the enemy's lie is that I cannot possibly be moving forward, because I am in fact, standing still.

II Chronicles 20:17 says… *"Ye shall not need to fight in this battle: set yourselves, stand ye still, and see the salvation of the LORD with you, O Judah and Jerusalem: fear not, nor be dismayed; to morrow go out against them: for the LORD will be with you."*

In this instance, God told Judah and the inhabitants of Jerusalem to stand still. There was still a battle – yes. However, they did not actually have to fight. Had they disobeyed and panicked after God spoke to them, they would have been annihilated. They were not strong enough by themselves to go up against the 'great multitude' that was headed their way. Even though they had received word from God, His word said "tomorrow go out against them". Therefore, until such time, they simply had to wait and do nothing. God had to let Judah, the inhabitants of Jerusalem and King Jehoshaphat know that the enemy was coming up against God and not the people, thus it was in fact His battle, and not anyone else's. The translation is "Step aside. I've got this…it's my fight. You can get somewhere and just be still."

When you are 'in Christ', and He is moving, you don't have to. When He lets us know that the battle belongs to him, then we don't need to fight. When He is fighting, we don't need to. When He's mobile, we are allowed to be still. When He is still, and instructs us to move, then we are allowed to move. Because God is victory, when we walk in Him, we are victorious automatically. He is progressive. Therefore, we are automatically progressive by association. God is certainly a God of motion; so then, because He is mobile, we likewise move in the motion of His spirit and not in the *e*motion of our own spirit.

He told them that there was no need for them to fight this particular battle; but rather, that they should stand still. They were obedient. They worshipped God for what He promised He would do. We miss out on a lot of big things – like inheritance and such - because we ourselves refuse to stand still. God mentions here, that the salvation of the Lord is 'with you'. The victory of the Lord was with them. Well, who can really ask for anything more? 'Now, the salvation of the Lord is with you', and you are in Christ…sounds like a preset fight to me.

Being in Christ, and seeing the salvation of the Lord with you sounds like a double entendre. People think that standing still makes you weak. In fact, it is more like just the opposite, where standing still makes you stronger. *Standing* still helps you to reassess, recollect and recover. *Being* still and standing in one place gives you a better outlook and helps you to withstand the winds and the storm – regardless of the forecast. Stillness gives you more than just sight. It also gives you insight, foresight, and literally myopic vision! And, when you can see better, you are much more spiritually competitive. You are able to contend with the wiles of the enemy. In short, standing still allows you to be more focused than anything.

Have you ever been to the ballet or seen a ballerina spin? She is so well poised and has such a sophisticated and defined motion that she could really appear to be still. At this point, she has mastered her motion. The mastery of motion is the true art of stillness. Consider the earth rotating on its axis. It turns or rotates once within a 24-hour period. That's equivalent to moving at 1000 miles per hour. The earth's rotation is what gives us night and day as well as our four seasons. Yet, we can't feel its movement. It is awesome when you think about it – that the earth spins at such a rate of speed that we cannot tell there is any motion at all!

On the journey of discovery, we seek to find out who we are and where we are going. Sometimes we go all through life without ever having taken the time to find out who we really are. Some today still seek to find their purpose. From the beginning of life, we are shaped and molded, encouraged and sometimes even discouraged by parents, grandparents, caregivers, educators, spiritual leaders and others. Some of us make a decision while in high school, college or later to work towards becoming who we would like to become. Some work towards this end - spiritually. Some – naturally. Others work towards this end in both the natural and the spiritual. However, there are those of us who have never taken the time to stop and find out who we really are or where we are going. Don't despair. There is hope. Take the time to be still and answer the questions at the end of this segment. Though simple, perhaps you have never been asked to pen who you are on paper. We are here on this earth so I think it only fitting and proper that we know that we have been selected for a specific work and purpose. Moreover, if it takes standing still in order to etch out your purpose, then so be it.

According to the Random House Dictionary, stillness is the absence of motion. It is the state of no motion or movement. I am hopeful that this reading will take you to a discovery point – where you are challenged to stand still and see, be still and know, keep still and do. And, in so doing, we can discover who God is, who we are, and how we live, move and have our being – in Him. Doing while being still may seem somewhat oxymoronic, but we should all be able to take an *active* part in being still. Because what we do is often indicative of who we are, and because we always have a *choice* in how we handle ourselves, then we must know that when we are truly standing in stillness, we are never ever stuck.

Manna Moment

Standing still serves as an internal mobilizer; as keeping still serves as your stabilizer

Introductory questions and thoughts for discussion

1. Describe the person you see when you look in the mirror. Who are you?

2. Now describe the person you would like to see when you look in the mirror.

3. Compare and contrast the difference between who you are now and who you would like to become.

4. What steps will you take to get you from where you are to where you need to be?

5. What do you believe has been the hindrance for you not having reached your goal/s?

6. List some goals that you have set and reached up until the point where you are currently.

We must set new and realistic goals and challenges for ourselves every day and parallel the goals set, with the action it should take to attain these goals. Otherwise, we go through life traveling on an average ticket failing to recognize that we are first class citizens in Christ. You cannot have a coach-like mindset with first class goals.

CHAPTER ONE

Taking a Stand

The priority of taking a stand has to be discipline. There is an order to discipline. Order establishes control; and control is needed after having taken a stand. Control allows you to maintain your stance. There are those who believe that discipline is not the key factor in stillness. On the contrary, consider that it takes complete trust in the Lord in order to let Him hold you in his arms in trying times. Taking the stand to be still says that you have to remain focused on your stillness while life continues to happen to you. One's mind has to be completely disciplined in order to will your confidence over to a God that you cannot physically see. In hours of darkness – when we are literally ready to throw in the towel, God says to us, "Let me bear your need." We will find that when we are in a position of trust with God, we will give our need to Him and allow Him to rock us to sleep.

Taking a stand says that no matter what is going on around you, stillness is on the menu as the order of the day. Stillness is only as still as the choice you make to become it. Have you ever been in a place of peace? Peace puts us in a place of stillness. Sometimes peace comes after calamity. Sometimes peace can come prior to a storm. Other times, God will give us *His* peace right in the middle of some of our storms. How extraordinarily deafening for the commanding voice of God to authorize even peace to be still…as if peace by itself weren't still enough?!

We seem to spend our lives moving towards Christ. But coming into maturity usually brings us not just closer to Christ, but places us directly in him…as long as that is truly the place where we choose to be. The more we come into Christ, the more still we are - as only by, through and in him – are we able to exist and stand complete in Him. Once we are truly in Christ it becomes much easier for us to stand still. It's kind of like being a baby again. We know that if babies are hungry or thirsty, they are usually fed and given drink; bathed, changed and sometimes rocked to sleep. In either case and for the most part, their need is met. And at the end of the day, once they are resting and asleep, they are still. Even a toddler who knows how to walk, but has that desire to be picked up and loved knows that they are usually protected and are typically at peace in the arms of a parent. In fact, that is the place where they seem to be most comfortable… in the loving arms of a parent or care-giver. It just seems to be more problematic for an adult to get it - that we can go to God for everything …no matter what the need may be.

Taking a stand is declaring verbally first, that you are willing to not only stand but also withstand your personal time of testing. Often we are bold enough to stand up at the beginning of our storms with no problem – vowing to be still standing when the storm is over. But some of us have had some storms to come that have either literally knocked us flat on the ground or knocked the wind out of us. Nevertheless, I am so grateful to have been cast down by some of my storms, but not destroyed in them.

Think about when we were toddlers just learning how to walk. If you can't remember, just picture a toddler learning how to walk. To watch a baby finally grasp even just standing up is interesting. They are sometimes wobbly, and often fall down after having stood – due to the excitement of this new accomplishment. If standing still were that easy, I probably would not be writing this book. Even after having learned how to walk, the toddler usually will go back to a position of crawling. Then when he reaches something that he can grip and hold on to, he will use that thing to pull himself up and stand again – being still long enough to regain balance, refocus and try again.

Likewise, we (having been new in Christ) have often fallen down when we've gotten weak on our feet. But the newness experience in Christ was still so exciting to us that we would just get back up feeling strong and invincible as if we had never even fallen. When we first knew Christ, it was a new relationship. We were in agreement with Him. What could go wrong? The difference between being with God and being with man is this: When you are in a relationship with someone, that other person is human. God though, is divine. With humankind, when something goes wrong, both you and that person need to go and get help for a situation. When we are in a relationship with God, we need to recognize that He IS the help. (Psalms 46:1) And, our need is instantly met. Even though sometimes our situation may be in our today, we have to continue to walk to meet up with our tomorrow until we experience the abundant victory.

There is a phrase that over the years, has kept me going: "Don't worry about tomorrow… God is already there." Once I had heard that statement, it became a declarative for me and I started living those words. For some of us, our tomorrow is next week. For others, it's next month. And for others still – it's years to come. "…*weeping may endure for a night, but joy cometh in the morning.*" (Psalms 30:5) But regardless of when tomorrow is for you, or when your 'morning' is, what an assurance to not have to worry about tomorrow. God somehow steps into all of our tomorrows, fixes our issues, comes back into our todays, and lets us know that not only is everything going to be alright, but that everything is *already* alright because God has the fix-it power to erase my yesterday, calm my today, and command my tomorrow. He is our fix-it master! And while things that took place in our yesterday might not have been things that we would've liked to have happened, I am convinced that a lot of our todays and even many more of our tomorrows are blessed beyond measure due to calamitous activities that took place in our yesterdays. Our todays are witness to our yesterdays; and our yesterdays are undoubtedly predetermined to shape our tomorrows. So on those days and in those times when just about everything seems to go wrong, we can take some comfort in knowing that those situations still prepare us for *other* situations. We cannot go through life without look-back knowledge and appreciation of the place from whence we have emerged. Our yesterdays are in place to remind us that we should not forget.

There was always the abundant excitement that God could do anything – when we were first saved. Anything! How is it then, after having not just been in a good relationship but in a God–relationship and having seen God bring us out of situations time and time again, that we doubt that God can bring us out of an even greater situation? He is that same God. If He did it before, He is more than able to do it again. If He brings you to a test, He will bring you through the test. If He guides you to a place, He will provide for you *in* that place. If He leads you to it, He will see you through it. Every storm is designed to end. Yes. Some storms are disastrous and unfortunately, there have been and will continue to be some casualties of certain storms. But, with proper planning and preparation, we can survive the storms. Often we do have time to cushion ourselves from the storms blow, but we neglect the warning signs and instructions to evacuate. Intentionally missing instructions can be costly.

How many times have you purchased an item and couldn't wait to get home, get it out of the box? I have done this plenty of times, and was so excited to use the item; I just put the directions to the side and start trying to put the item together. I thought, "How hard can this be?" Well, I've had to many times go back after trying to put parts together, take everything apart and start all over again because I neglected to follow the directions. Thus, the equipment either didn't function at its maximum capacity; functioned improperly or sometimes not at all.

GOT TEXT?

The same is true during a spiritual storm. During our storms, our instructions may not come to us via the internet, radio or TV, but God's people do receive text messaging! There's a great big book that we have. It is full of text and has an abundance of messages for us. On any given day or time, we can open up the bible to just about any page, and receive a word from the Lord. That's unequivocally ultimate text messaging! IAFT...that's text for It's all *for* the good! (Romans 8:28) *"And we know that all things work together for good to them that love God, to them who are the called according to his purpose."* We so very often hear "It's all good!" But as a child of God, I recognize that really, it isn't always *all* good, but I can certainly appreciate that – when you love God, and when you are one of 'the called', it's definitely all *for* the good.

Remember that trust factor that babies have while being rocked in a parent's arms? They don't know any better. The trust is automatic. It's innate. Without a care in the world, they just trust. I suppose it's because they don't know how NOT to trust. When we grow up...that is to say mature, our trust in the Lord should also be grown up. Somehow, we forget that we should *still* trust God all the more - as little children trust those who have authority and rule over them. Without any knowledge of how they will be fed, children just know that they will be. Without any knowledge of where the food comes from, there is a certain level of expectancy that children have in their parents and those who have rule over them. In fact, we are still God's children. And, we ought to want to exercise a certain level of faith…child-like faith. Graduated faith that says that my need will be met because I have a supplier where I get *all* of my help. Psalms 121.1-2 says *"I will lift up mine eyes unto the hills, from whence cometh my help; my help cometh from the Lord, which made heaven and earth."* God is our provider. He is the ultimate service provider. And the nice thing about our service provider is that He gives us options. We have many options. Talk about a plan! As long as we belong to God, He will have the total rule over us, grant us peace in our circumstances, and keep us as still as He deems necessary…for our good.

When we've fallen, we need to remember that we can get up. We have an anchor in Christ. It is so much fun to watch the child pull up with a spark of determination in her eyes. She is transitioning from one position to another. She's simply and literally taking a stand – and usually mighty proud of it. We likewise should use whatever means necessary to pull ourselves up so that we can take a stand and transition from the place where we *were* to the place we are trying to go. There's a saying, 'If you don't stand for something, you'll fall for anything.' If you have to stand for something, you may as well at least stand up for yourself. If you aren't standing, how can you offer help to someone else who has fallen? Stand up for something you believe in. And, that something might as well be *a* some-one. And that someone might as well be you standing with total hope and complete trust in Christ. So please stand and remain standing.

Taking a Stand

Imagine standing completely still without flinching in the middle of the floor for about fifteen minutes. Think of how hard that would be for most people. After a lifetime of running about here, there and everywhere and following a daily routine… it's really hard to stand still. I have finally learned that the art of standing still begins with taking a stand. If your brain doesn't tell your legs to stand in one place and hold completely still, you likely will *not* stand still. You really will need to be disciplined enough to *allow* this to happen. Standing still takes disallowing the things around you to consume you. What I am literally suggesting is that you take no action. We are so prone to react and respond immediately to the things that take place around us, that this particular task – although there isn't much involved – could actually be quite tough to accomplish. But, I promise you that when you begin to stand still, after a time, the things around you will somehow in a way, lay dormant, and something within you, will begin to move. So then it's not just standing still, but rather, the art thereof.

Imagine what goes on while you are sleeping…all of the action that takes place in your mind and in your dreams while your body lays still. Often, it is as if your mind is having a party and your body isn't invited. Again, art. Your body doesn't even know that the party is going on. It just lies listlessly in wait…until the mind is finished with its running about… and has released itself to reconnect with the body, and released the body to resume its normal activities. And then you wake up.

When we are at our worse, God is at His best. There have been times when I have felt like I was at my worse; and I now realize that this is such a good place to be. It's a good time to be used by God. It took me a little more than a minute to realize that there's real truth to this. It is so hard for us sometimes to see that the essence of who God is, is often realized when we need Him the most. When we are in need of God we are desirable to Him. Often, this is when we pour out our souls and render ourselves helpless; thereby giving God permission to operate on our behalf. He designed us to be in need of Him. Our desire then should be so in need *of* Him that we give our need *to* Him, and He in return will '*supply all [our] need according to His riches in glory.*' (Phil 4:19) We need Him the most usually when we are down and out and seemingly out of options. This is when we fellowship with him… in our sickness and often not so much in our health… more in our downs rather than our ups…usually in our valleys as opposed to our mountains.

Manna Moment

A voluntary yield toward stillness could lead to a mandatory move of God

Psalms 46:10 Says, *Be still, and know that I am God: I will be exalted among the heathen; I will be exalted in the earth.*

I'M RUNNING FOR MY LIFE!

I remember when I was in elementary school at the tender age of eight. It was just about the end of recess when from a distance I saw a dog running towards me. From the looks of it, the dog was coming directly to me. Well, my family did not have any pets. Moreover, dog might be man's best friend, but it certainly wasn't mine. I was terrified. When I realized that the dog was coming in my direction, I panicked, made like a plane moving on a runway and I took off! Everywhere I ran the dog was close behind. I ran around the monkey bars, the slides, the see saw, the swings and just kept on circling the open space of the playground – which was huge. It caused such a commotion, with all my crying and screaming that there was a hush over the playground.

I recall all eyes on me as I continued to cry and run for my life. I cried so hard that my vision became blurry. By now, no one was playing on the field. Every eye was on me…students and teachers - alike. I heard many people talking but after awhile, it became one voice. I couldn't make it out at first (I had other things to worry about), but I soon heard what everyone was chanting: "Pattie, stop running. Just stop running!" Why were they telling me not to run? I *had* to run. This beast was after me. Why was everyone on the sidelines? Why was no one coming to my rescue? How come no one would call the dog away from me or come and get him? "He won't bite you!" was all they kept saying. Yeah, right. That was easy for all of them to say. They weren't the ones running from this ferocious animal.

Well, as it turns out, I simply could no longer run. I was out of breath, out of ideas, angry and pet-trified. So I finally stopped running. I remember thinking, 'This is it. This is the end! The dog will bite me and I would be maimed for life – if I even had any life left in me at all.' Suddenly, exhausted and frustrated, I stopped running and stood still right where I was and braced myself to be eaten up by this crazy dog while the whole playground watched. And what do you know? I'll be doggone! Exactly that: the dog was gone. When I stood still, he kept going! He didn't want me after all. Wow. Apparently he was only playing with me and thought that because I was running, I was also playing with him. Well, needless to say that my little ordeal was school talk for probably several weeks. But what a valuable lesson I learned that day. And, that day is as vivid in my mind today as it was when it happened then.

How many times in our lives have we opened our mouths and later wished we hadn't? How many times have we been instructed to be silent but instead we developed the 'couldn't-help-its' and the 'just can't stops', opened our mouths and ruined a perfectly tolerable situation and then had to later apologize to a person and/or repent before God? There have been times when I knew I was right, but had to be still AND silent and painfully smile through it all. It's a hurtful thing to know that you know you are right but can't really say anything; or to be told you're wrong when you know you're right. It is just human nature for us to want to speak up for ourselves and even fight. But taking a stand in Christ means that we don't need to fight. Why? Because Jesus Christ is our advocate and He will defend us. When we allow Christ to defend us, whether or not we win or lose, we still Stand in victory – as long as we allow Christ to plead our case.

This may seem like a hard thing to grasp; but this is because in our minds, when we think about being attacked, we immediately pull out the war paint, weapons, and begin to gear up to fight. Why is it that we no longer take our burden to the Lord and leave it there? Do we even consult God anymore regarding our next steps? How do we know which position we should hold in battle?

Often there isn't even a need to fight because that battle is often not our own. This is why we can appear to have suffered a loss and still be victorious. This is why we can be sick unto death but still living like nobody's business. It's why the enemy can have us in the morgue but we're still breathing. Often, when we try to get in the situation, we mess it up. Standing still allows our enemy to walk right on by us.

Manna Moment

While movement is counter-productive to stillness, stillness will often provoke movement.

When we have an advocate, most of the times we are instructed not to speak. Our advocate speaks on our behalf. What a hard thing to do. I've been in court before and instructed not to speak because I had an attorney who would speak on my behalf. Keeping silent was such a hard thing for me because I wanted to tell my story. You know how we do… "Well see, what had happened was…" My will was certainly not to be still. My will was to speak, because I felt like I knew the story better than the advocate. After all, I was there when the incident happened, and he wasn't. But I have also found that when you have an advocate to speak for you, you have to be able to put your trust in him/her. So, by still choosing to speak for yourself, an undeserving enemy could win your case. Even though it is a hard thing to do sometimes, resisting the will to speak helps us. Often, being still and keeping silent helps us to be victorious. Sometimes we just talk entirely too much!

God will always have an advocate for us. I recall many incidents growing up and while in school - where and when I had an advocate. In high school and unbeknownst to me, there were incidents that would take place - where before the school day was out, a student by the name of Sherry would show up out of nowhere to get the '411' and find out the who, what, when, where, why and the how of it all. Sometimes she had found out that there were situations that involved me; and there she would be – in the mix – at my defense. When all of this would happen, I never really saw it for what it was. I was still trying to figure out what it was. I later learned that Sherry was in fact assigned to me; and I – to her.

Sometimes it was downright annoying that as soon as something would go down at school, there was Sherry on the scene asking questions like "What happened?" and "Who did it?" and "Where are they now?" and "What do you want me to do to them?" For whatever reason, Sherry always felt the need to protect me. And at that particular time, I didn't feel a need to have my own private security guard. It was as if she always showed up at a crime scene to investigate prior to any crime even taking place; which is now somewhat funny because she went on to become a commendable police officer. Not only that, but she's my dearest friend 'til this day…and I'm happy to say - *still* an advocate and protector of sorts! I am ever so grateful that our paths crossed in this life.

BE STRONG

When we can find out what those things are that make us weak, we can eliminate them from our lives and become stronger. We ought also to recognize that there is an abundance of strength in our weakness. Our weakness compels us to find strength in the power source – our Lord and savior – Jesus Christ. (II Corinthians 12:10) *"Therefore I take pleasure in infirmities, in reproaches, in necessities, in persecutions in distresses for Christ's sake: for when I am weak, then am I strong."*

Strongholds make for weak stances. So, if we are to stand strong, stand long and stand still, we must determine what the strongholds are in our lives, and pull them down. (II Corinthians 10:3-6) *"For though we walk in the flesh, we do not war after the flesh: (For the weapons of our warfare are not carnal, but mighty through God to the pulling down of strong holds;) Casting down imaginations, and every high thing that exalteth itself against the knowledge of God, and bring into captivity every thought to the obedience of Christ; revenge all disobedience, when your obedience is fulfilled."*

Knowing that God is our advocate lends us to a place spiritually, where we can stand the test, take the stand and stand trial. Not only is God our defense, but He is also our judge. As well, our willingness to take the stand says that we are able to stand still. Getting to the point where we are strong enough to withstand our tests will get us to the place where we are still enough to stand trial.

Manna Moment:

Standing still gives us a great view of the future!

End of chapter questions and thoughts for discussion

1. Are you strong enough now to withstand an unforeseen test?

2. Are you still enough to endure your current tests? If not, then do you see where being still could increase your survivability?

3. Give an example of something that makes you strong.

4. Give an example/s of something that makes you weak.

5. Include an example of something that makes you still.

6. Cite the differences or similarities (if any) of the answers to questions 3, 4, and 5.

When we can find out what those things are that make us still, we can – like vitamins – add them to our daily diet to balance us out.

CHAPTER TWO

NIGHT BLINDNESS

Manna Moment

In the darkness is where our level of faith is revealed

It is in the very moment that we freeze ourselves to watch what is going on in our own lives that we have the opportunity to establish what we want or will to happen in our future. This is outcome. Have you ever known someone to have night blindness? I have. The medical term for this is nyctalopia. In order for a doctor to determine what causes night blindness, the doctor has to perform a series of tests. This usually means they are unable to drive at nights. Their vision is usually very poor. The instruction to not drive at night comes from a medical practitioner. Typically, this person's vision is compromised by the darkness. As with all of us, objects that are usually quite easily seen in the day are not as visible in the night.

    Indeed, the danger of night blindness is that you could actually kill someone or you yourself could die by operating heavy equipment while unable to see with clarity. For too long, even though we have had sight, our vision has been impaired. God's people cannot afford to have spiritual night blindness. The enemy lurks in places where we can't physically see. So, because our sight doesn't work as well in the dark as it does in the light, this is when our vision has to kick in. *"For we wrestle not against flesh and blood, but against principalities, against powers, against the rulers of the darkness of this world, against spiritual wickedness in high places."* (Ephesians 6:12) We are usually weaker at nights. In addition, when it is time for us to settle down and retire for the night, the principalities, powers, and spiritual wickedness that dwell in the high places, seek us out to wreak havoc whenever and wherever they are able…even through our dreams…when we are vulnerable.

With those who have been medically diagnosed with night blindness, the eyes may merely have difficulty adjusting or adapting to the darkness. However, spiritual detachment of your retina could result in one losing his or her vision. Again, because we walk by faith and not by sight, then we recognize that our faith goes well beyond sight and actually produces vision. Funny, one can live without sight, but die without vision. And, where there is no vision, the people perish (Proverbs 29:18). Thus, sight is no longer in the equation. This is why even without sight, those who may be physically blind can still have vision. Vision gives sight to the blind. Through faith and with vision, we can still hope, see and do.

Manna Moment

One can live without sight, but die without vision

In fact, often it is better that we do not see certain situations directly. We would so totally freak out. Have you experienced a time when you were able to step back from your situation, get a total view of the circumstance or test at hand, and just lost it? "How am I going to do this God?" we might ask. Or "Are you kidding? I can't do this by myself!" Well, no…you can't do it by yourself! Neither could the children of Israel cross through the Red Sea over to the other side without Moses' rod of hope and faith of steal. Therefore, when and as we are tested amidst the darkest of times, we should always allow our light of faith to kick in and continue to guide us through each test. And, we are then no longer the victims of blindness – night or otherwise. *"But if we hope for that which we see not, then do we with patience wait for it."* (Romans 8:25)

Now imagine that you have spiritual nyctalopia. If you have spiritual night blindness, there's a mild film or coating over your pupil. For now, I will call that film, a distraction. Night blindness is not total blindness. Ones' vision is impaired only at night. Someone who has night blindness can typically still see fine as long as there is daylight. And, driving when there's daylight is not a strain either. However, at night, straining to see could actually damage your vision to the point where it is irreparable. And straining to see at night could further impair your vision in the day. Forcing yourself to see at night is like straining to see in the darkness. In Christ, we don't need to strain to see at night or in the darkness. If we are still, we can close our eyes and always see the rescuing hand of God – careful to not allow any distraction to come our way. The sun's light may blind us, but as long as we are powered by the Son, our vision is not impaired. And, as long as Jesus Christ, the Son of God, empowers us…that is to say, as long as we have an efficacious relationship with Christ, our vision will undoubtedly stay intact.

The real danger of night blindness seems to occur when an individual is mobile. If this individual were to be still and remain in his stillness, night blindness may not necessarily be the diagnosis. Our words become life, and that life that we live has become a light to and for others. So then, if we're not walking in the word, then we aren't walking in the light and we will remain in darkness. Because the light shines in darkness and the darkness doesn't understand the light. (John 1:5)

No matter how dark things get in your life, if we walk as lights, then those who are in the dark will never be able to understand us – if and when they are living in the darkness. Until they choose to come towards and eventually into the light, they will continue to see us as 'different' than they. And in fact, we are. In Christ, we are like a city that is set on a hill. There's no way we can be hidden. If a light is in the darkness and ceases to shine, then it ceases to be a light. No matter where we are in life, when our light no longer shines, we are of no effect to the darkness around us. Rather, we become the darkness. We are unable to speak on behalf of light. Remember, we have been chosen. We are illuminators, not blenders. Affecting change in the atmosphere is what we do. It just comes with the territory. And what an awesome privilege that is!

I am reminded of Saul as he was on his way to Damascus and he was blinded by a certain light. Even though the event took place at midday, the light was so bright it knocked him down to the ground. The whole event happened so that others might be converted from darkness to light. And even though it was broad day light, his life had a dark tone to it.

(Read Acts 9:1-9) Saul had to go to conversion school.

Declaratively, we are to light the way so that those who are in darkness can see our light and give glory to our God. (Matthew 5:16) *"Let your light so shine before men, that they may see your good works, and glorify your Father which is in heaven."* Spiritually speaking, night blindness really could be a great gift of faith.

When our sight fails, our faith is equipped to take us the rest of the way. So if you happen to find yourself in a particular test, and you just can't see your way out, then try to faith your way out! This is when faith goes from being a noun to becoming a verb. You have to realize that faith is not just what you have, but it's also what you do. So sometimes, you will just have to walk it out in your now in order to see it in your then.

Why do so many Christians who are walking in the light – think that there is something for them hidden in the dark places when God has brought us out of darkness? (I Peter 2:9) *"But ye are a chosen generation, a royal priesthood, an holy nation, a peculiar people; that ye should shew forth the praises of him who hath called you out of darkness into his marvelous light."*

There have been many who have run into the proverbial world to get a taste of what was there, and didn't make it from the darkness back into the light to tell about it. Yet there is something so mysteriously wanting about the dark that we Christians sometimes want to do a drive-by on the wild side just to see what is going on over there. This want generally happens when our lights get dim. But even a dim light can still be seen in the darkness. If we stay in the darkness with a dim light, eventually we will blend with the darkness once our shine goes out. So even though we might think that we're unrecognizable and we've blended into the dark, our light still shines internally – warning us (and others) that we are in the wrong place. Thus, out of place and out of sync with the light. If we are out of sync, then we are still in danger and can be broadsided and blinded by the night without an external light to guide us. When our light gets dim our faith to see must kick in to guide us the rest of the way. Some of us have become so immune to the darkness that we no longer serve as lights and are unable to draw men unto Christ, but rather, unto ourselves. Remember what happened Lucifer? Okay. Enough said.

Manna Moment:

Remember that faith is the vehicle through which sight is produced

At one point in my life, so many things had taken place that I reached a place that I ended up having to say "have faith, will travel!" I actually tapped into other resources before I tapped into my faith. There is something so important that we miss when it comes to faith. When we have it, we can literally go anywhere. Both faith and sight are set up as parallel streets. Sight often has faith built in, but doesn't know it; so sight goes out on the town on its own as cocky as ever - thinking that as long as it can see, it needs nothing else. Sight travels but is limited in its scope and view because it can only see straight ahead. I know that faith can pick up on some things that sight can miss.

THE SIXTH SENSE

Sight believes that it has everything it needs to survive. That is why I am so grateful for faith… the sixth sense. Faith is the only entity that acts as a stand-alone sense. As the sixth sense, faith needs no directives from any of the other senses. Faith is an innate built-in sense that just takes you there. It is only activated by a soul command…a command that always kicks in when the time is right. Unfortunately, we typically wait until we reach a point of desperation and have exhausted all of our other resources: family, friends, etc., before we admit that we have nothing else. While faith sits in the waiting room of a hospital as next of kin - waiting for sight to be declared immobile or dead all the while saying "I'm here…you can use me." Or "Pick me! Pick me!" However, a very anemic sight often ignores faith.

Faith is never disobedient. When you tell it "Let's do this," it moves. When you say, "I don't know where I'm going to land, but we are getting ready to take off!" It will not only follow, but concurrently, it will lead. It will follow instructions instinctively; and then position itself ahead of you because it has to go full throttle before fear (or any other distraction/s) has an opportunity to take over. Both faith and fear have the ability to delete each other; so we need to be certain that our faith leads us. Sometimes when faith says 'I can do this,' sight chimes in with "Well, I just don't see how it's going to happen!" Faith should always be the believer's first choice.

> *"But if we hope for that we see not, then do we with patience wait for it." (Romans 8:25)*

Faith is a true servant-leader. It serves us by following our command, but then leads us by taking over once we are noticeably tired. The only catch is that it is voice-activated. We must be able to command our faith to move the mountains in our lives. Faith is a query-answering, frontward-thinking, forward-stepping, by-force taking, call-answering, no nonsense, hassle-free sense. It is a call and response sense. It is optimized by and responds to your call. It is as if faith is personified. You become the commander and faith is the orderly. Faith responds to all of your commands. It is simple. You call and faith answers. Whatever we put out in the atmosphere, faith follows our words and serves as a seasoning agent. When we begin to make declarations that will shift our position in the atmosphere, our faith begins to ramp up – gearing itself and preparing for takeoff; because no sooner do the words leave our mouths, our faith forges ahead and acts as a cushion to our dreams and a carrier to our visions. Faith's personification says that the thing we were called to do is like a military assignment. If we could only think of faith as a person, and learn to lean on it, follow its lead and trust it, then we would be better served.

Manna Moment:

Our faith is not powered by sight, but our vision is empowered by our faith

When your sight is gone, it is as if God intuitively gives you more…like a substitute. Your hearing is probably fortified, or your sense of smell is incredibly enhanced. There is another innate ability that you have that seemingly overcompensates for the sense that one was not born with. I have made a special notation on children in particular who are autistic. It seems as though children born into autism – while they might lack a particular skill set and/or possibly even one of their senses, there seems to be consistency in the thought that the area in which they are talented is magnified and often even maximized. They are seemingly exponentially gifted with their talents.

Here is a good thing about night blindness: For those of you - of us – who can spiritually not see at night, please look at this as a gift. Let me explain. Those who have night blindness must needs rely on faith! If you happen to be spiritually blinded, then your faith has to guide you through whatever situation you may be in. In other words, you may not be able to see just how God is going to operate for you in a particular situation, but you have the faith to believe that God will bring you out of it. People who have physically lost their sight, need to regain hope in one of their other senses. So in this sense, faith can be substituted for one of the senses. In fact, faith can be substituted for any of the major senses. It is a direct substitute for sight. It has the ability to see what we don't. Faith also has the ability to hear things that go beyond our human audible capacity. Take for example something such as our passions. Faith indirectly hears what our heart speaks, but it waits for our permission before it takes flight. Through our actions, when our speak is gone, faith operates as a tongue. It has a language all its own. They say that actions speak louder than words, but faith speaks even louder than actions. Our faith actually brings us to our actions. Even our sense of smell can be heightened by our faith. Why, with faith as a replaced sense, we can smell favor from miles away.

What?!

Manna Moment

Negativity deactivates our faith

Even our sense of taste is heightened by our level of faith. Have you ever wanted something so badly that you could taste it? At that time, faith is so powerful that it can take you to a place where you can see yourself in position doing what you do or desire to do in the future. But if you can see it in the future so clearly that you can taste it in your now, then you've already crossed over from little faith, and have accessed another level of faith. Then touch…What an awesomely powerful sense. For this, I can appreciate dreams and visions. If I have the audacity to see with my little faith, let alone touch it with my faith, I can certainly cross over into great faith and get it! We have to start seeing the mobility and travel-ability of our faith. When we do, then we will stop checking our faith – as we do our luggage, and always take it with us as a carry-on no matter where we go. Truth be told, our "carry-on" is sometimes left, but rarely lost because we have taken the opportunity with care to carry it with us… along with those items we deem "valuable" on whatever faith trip we take. We like to have items of value near us or on our person. Faith should also be put in that category…in our 'carry-on' at all times. We should value our faith with our life. Doing this will ensure that our faith becomes us. No matter how discouraging a place we are in – in life, carrying our faith with us at all times will ensure that it – along with other important and valued items– doesn't get lost along the way. If only we can learn to close our eyes (and often our mouths), and open our faith and lean on the master – our Lord and savior Jesus Christ, then faith can take us wherever we need to go. Faith has the capacity to lead us throughout our life's entirety.

RE-USE

We can go green with our faith! Where we would normally have limited means, reusing our faith can create additional resources for us. If tires can be re-treaded, plastic bottles can be recycled, then our faith should be no different. We can use it again and again. Reuse reduces cost. When you have a bottle of water that is finished, and you choose to refill and reuse it time after time, it is cost efficient in the long run. It's just as economical for us to reuse our faith by refilling it. The more we use our faith, the better equipped we are to get to the next level of faith. It is like reward points or frequent flyer miles. The bonus is that through faith, we can *see* the benefits. The benefit of reusing your faith over and over again is that it perpetuates your blessing scale. Great tests produce great levels of faith; and great levels of faith produce even greater testimonies.

Manna Moment

What we say with our mouths affect the direction of our feet

Allow me for a moment, to take you on a sight-light journey. The journey is sight-less and not sight-free. This is because your faith can see obstacles that you with your naked eye may never see. Here, faith serves as a protector to you. Faith foresees obstacles but it also combats, counteracts and serves as a conquering agent for any and everything that you may go through. How is it that even those without sight can have enough faith to push through their physical disability? How is it that without sight, one can still be a victor rather than a victim? Hebrews 11:6 *"But without faith, it is impossible to please him: for he that cometh to God must believe that he is, and that he is a rewarder of them that diligently seek him."*

With faith as the traveling vehicle of choice, God is well pleased when we choose this vehicle as our life-mode of transportation. Faith is close to God. We must be strong enough to carry faith with us at all times so that when we are weak, the strength of our faith will carry us. Faith not only walks us throughout various life avenues, it also drives us into opportunities and destinies that would not otherwise be realized. With faith, our dark tests can produce well-lit rewards. After all, our faith shines best when we are tested. Additionally, a true test of our faith happens in the darkest of times – albeit naturally or spiritually. When there is light, we can see straight ahead of us for as far as the eyes can see. While the darkness can momentarily suspend our ability to see, our faith will produce enough light to see our way through any circumstance. How can a dark place produce light? When we get to this level of faith, it becomes voice-activated. What we see is often challenging to our faith in that our sight can tell our mind, "We can't do this." However, faith says that nothing is impossible. Therefore, it forges ahead victoriously and triumphantly.

Manna Moment

How well we see in the darkness could determine how well we walk in the light

FAITH IS THE NEW SIGHT

Retinal Detachment is when the retina becomes separated from its underlying supportive tissue. The retina cannot function when these layers are detached, and unless it is reattached soon, permanent vision loss could result. Because of this, there are times when what you see is not always what you get. Spiritually, the enemy sometimes gives us a picture of everything that is going on in our lives. All of the 'worse case scenarios' for our trials and tests, and wants us to believe that what we are seeing is our life as it should be; and that the picture in front of us is an accurate and actual snapshot of our life. It isn't. He's a liar. The things we see at night are obscure – at best. For those of us who have matured in the things we see and do, faith has taken over and become the new sight. Old sight says what you see is what you get. New faith says 'Even what you are unable to see, you can God-will it and *still* get it – if you believe.' New faith says 'If I can think it, I can have it and some more.' The blessing in night blindness is that if you have it, you are forced in a sense, to capitalize on the day when you have light. And work while it is day…while the light is present to lead your vision with precision.

When we reach a certain level, we recognize and see things in a totally different light. (1 Corinthians 13:11) *When I was a child, I spake as a child, I understood as a child, I thought as a child: but when I became a man, I put away childish things.* There are certain things that only come with time. There are things that children do because of their level of immaturity. Adults often expect children to do, act and be a certain way, but often they are just not there…which is why they have to be taught…which is why *we* have to be taught. God is so amazingly awesome, that he meets us where we are. Moreover, He does not expect us to respond from a place where we aren't. He meets us precisely where we are and then expects a response on that level. And, from that point on, we are taught and then expected to respond differently per each subsequent level we reach. 'Those who know better, do better.'

Maturity is a wonderful and splendid thing. It allows us to wait but not want. In that the Lord is our Shepherd, we ought to be wanting of nothing. As progressive as our God is, only when we are still can we truly experience an abounding movement of God. Waiting without wanting isn't easy, but it is a necessary part of the shedding process. It also affords us not only sight, but also vision. While sight is the ability to see, vision is the capability to see way beyond. Sight allows us to see what is in and around our area and space, and vision speaks louder than sight because it tells us that we are able to see things outside of the typical human scale.

Consider and compare the following:

SIGHT	VISION
Sight sees	Vision sees beyond
Sight prepares for now	Vision plans for later
Sight is silent	Vision speaks
Sight judges	Vision predicts
Sight enhances	Vision enables
Sight illuminates	Vision identifies

Sight deals with the khronos; the chronologies of things in your life as you see them... Vision deals with the 'set time' or kairos of things present and things to come, and also shows you how drastically different those same things can be in just one moment in time; or just how much more differently those same things can look in the future.

If we can take just one moment to deal with how we cross over into a different dimension. This crossover, or transition, is monumentalized when khronos meets kairos. Imagine the things you know to be in your now – meeting up with the things you desire in your future. We think of destiny as something we are to become or some place we are to be in the future. Thus, we strive continuously every day of our lives – often reaching our goals, but never reaching our supposed destiny, because we don't define them early enough to aspire towards them. When, if we are to set goals and actually reach them, we have in fact 'destinied' with that or those particular goals.

Manna Moment

*Sight shows your temperament.
Vision reveals your testimony*

Crossing over into that different dimension of that one moment when khronos meets kairos is like that the moment when sight meets vision...that moment when the things that we see, connect with the things that we have envisioned to become...is like a moment of epiphany/utopia. Okay, here's perhaps a better example: Think of a solar eclipse... Think of the transformation of a caterpillar into a butterfly... imagine that precise moment of transformation and what it feels like crossing over from one form into another... the changing of a tadpole into a frog... a seed into a plant...an embryo into a child... From a child into adulthood... Fact is, we're so busied with everything else going on around us that we often are unaware of the very things that take place right where we are...inside of us... When Saul experienced a transformation...it was so powerful his name was changed. When your present – in passing - meets up with your future in spite of your past, and pinnacles your promise, you have experienced a kairos moment. I would have to say though, that the ultimate moment of being "destinied" is when we in a flash, will transform to be with the Lord. (I Corinthians 15:52) *In a moment, in the twinkling of an eye, at the last trump: for the trumpet shall sound, and the dead shall be raised incorruptible, and we shall be changed.* WOW.

Manna Moment

Sight shows what your situation looks like in the natural. Vision reveals a very triumphant 'you' in the spiritual

If you are merely dealing with sight, then perhaps what you see is what you get. However, when you are dealing with vision, then one must recognize that what s/he sees is not always what s/he gets. Even 20/20 eyesight says I'm in a situation right now that I am unable to get out of and I can't see past where I am. But true vision says that regardless of where I am, I am in eyeshot of my future; and this situation will not stop me from achieving where I will be in the future or who I will become. With sight, it's all about where I am now because that is what I can see. With vision, it's about taking your ability, passion, and faith and forming *whatever* it is you desire. It's about God doing exceedingly and abundantly above all that we are able to ask or think. (Ephesians 3:20)

Manna Moment

Sight allows you to be all that you can see while Vision allows you to see all that you can be

Night Blindness

Here are two equations for the occasion:

$$\text{SIGHT} + \text{CIRCUMSTANCE/S} = \text{MOBILE MAYHEM}$$

$$\text{SIGHT} + \frac{\text{CIRCUMSTANCE/S}}{\text{FAITH (THE VISION ENHANCER)}} = \text{AN OPPORTUNITY FOR GOD TO MULTIPLY THE MAGNITUDE OF YOUR OUTCOME}$$

We cannot afford to look at our situations with our bare eyes. It will leave us running about without hope…trying to fix things all by ourselves. However, when we see our circumstances through vision, it then multiplies the strength of our stillness and produces purpose and fruition even *within* our circumstances.

When the scriptures say that we walk by faith and not by sight…please allow me to submit that there is no way that we can use our natural eyesight, and truly see things in the spirit. Our natural eyes are a great guide for us as we experience everyday life. But often our sight cannot handle the precision of vision nor the velocity of faith.

Manna Moment

Vision gives sight the permission to see what God has in store for your future

CHAPTER THREE

THE DANCE OF NIGHT STILLNESS

Manna Moment

Stillness is a platform for performance

It's pretty amazing, but for me, I have actually gotten more done while standing still than I have been able to accomplish while busy and running about. Busy and productive are two totally different things. So often we run here, there and everywhere – only to find at the end of the day, that we have accomplished absolutely nothing! But when we take a moment to stand in the stillness of our activities, we will often find that we are better able to understand the activities themselves. We may also find that true stillness deactivates a heightened level of stress. It can be administered as medication. In the life of the believer, a prescribed dose of *still* certainly could not hurt. Rather, it would help to put our individual lives in perspective, received direction and give us a vitamin-like boost.

Manna Moment

Stillness often reveals a movement of faith

The release of favor reigns mightily over the movement of faith. Since movement is motion…a change in position, I believe it is safe to say that where you are determines your next dance step. Because the night is mostly still, the decisions you make in the night could determine which position you end up in – in the morning. One wrong move at night could turn your morning into mourning. One Merriam Webster definition for stillness that I really like is: "A tactical or strategic shifting…" Have you ever woken up in the morning and have actually felt different…as if something took place while you were sleeping? Often while we sleep, things go *shift* in the night. We should be sure to document everything that we see at night. I am certain that some of those night sightings are not only on point, but also on purpose! Capturing what we see while we are still enables us to capitalize on the cadence of our future.

We often hear about destiny. Well, what exactly is it, and how do we get from where we are to our destiny or destination? Destiny is that place and position of peace and promise. Here's an equation for the occasion that might help to better define destiny for you. In short, destiny is not just where you are going, it's where you end up. You have the power to take a stand, be still and decide what you want to do, where you want to be, and move in the direction and the flow of your vision. The night gives us opportunity to write the vision and make it plain. (Habakkuk 2:2) *And the LORD answered me, and said, Write the vision, and make it plain upon tables, that he may run that readeth it.*

The day affords us the opportunity to take little steps towards that vision and dance until we get there.

$$\text{A VISION REALIZED} \times \text{A VISION WRITTEN} = \text{AN ACHIEVED DESTINATION}$$

When your goals, dreams and vision on paper become the place where you are, then the place where you stand becomes your destiny for that moment in time. What is the roadmap for our future? Once we recognize that our destiny is encapsulated in our gifting, we are more than half way there. Here is an equation for the occasion:

$$\text{GIFT} + \text{ACKNOWLDEGEMENT} = \text{ROOM}$$

STILL IN BUSINESS

I promise this is not a brainteaser. Once you acknowledge your gift, so much mental and spiritual growth happens in the stillness-sphere. The key to stillness here is mindset. (Romans 12:2) *"And be not conformed to this world, but be ye transformed by the renewing of your mind that you may prove what is that good, perfect and acceptable will of God."* Once we can change the way we think, we can delve into our gift/s, really acknowledge and understand it/them and know that it will make room for us wherever we are. It will often bless financially as well. Some of us are STILL working in the wrong field because we refuse to acknowledge and employ our true gifting. There's no room to doubt when it comes to our gifting.

God has put an order of completion out on my life. It's kind of like a contract. For me, this means that whatever I have set out to do in Him must be completed. Some of the things we set out to do are in fact things that we are supposed to do; but I've learned that we must move as we are told. Because some assignments are 'destinied' events are time sensitive, we can easily miss a window of opportunity slated for our now, but ended up being moved into our then – simply because we procrastinated.

Philippians 1:6 states, *"Being confident of this very thing, that he which has begun a good work in you will perform it until the day of Jesus Christ."* There are so many projects in my life that I have abandoned simply out of fear. Have you ever had a great idea – a hope, dream – or life project that you started to work on and just stopped? If so, why did you stop the project, abandon the dream, or give up on the hope? Giving up on these things will lead to our hopes and dreams to become endangered. I challenge you to revisit your desires and unshelve your passions and complete the movement. Something that can be annoying in music is an incomplete scale. Try singing the doe, re, mi, scale without the last note. Doe, re, mi, fa, so, la, ti, and no doe! What?! Just sing the last note!!! It's *your* scale… it's *your* movement. Complete the scale already! Finish what you start.

Some of the ideas that we start are or were meant to be our bread butter. So let's finish the race even if we walk or end up crawling to the finish line. If we are unfulfilled, it isn't God's fault. There have been so many things over the course of my life that I've started and left undone…from songs, to poetry, to new business ventures. Anything undone is good. Imagine biting into a slice of pound cake that appears done. And once you do, you taste the butter, eggs and flour – unmixed. Yuck! While the outside might have appeared to be appetizing, so much was raw and unfinished on the inside.

Whether or not you are taking the "stand-still" time to meditate, evaluate or seek answers, what a great opportunity to do some strategic planning! Sometimes silence is a great organizer. By allowing you to focus, silence can pinnacle your progress by merely allowing you to regroup and put things in a mental order. At a time when your thoughts are at best, full of extreme hyperactivity, silence and stillness can turn your ideas into big business. Stillness can actually help you to focus and finish a project. Some people could quite possibly *still* be in business - had they been still while in *business*.

Manna Moment

In stillness, our strength is not compromised
On the contrary, it is maximized

STILL IN MARRIAGE

There are times when we have need to be still in our relationships. Stillness in marriage will hold some marriages together. Stillness in marriage reminds us that it is not always the giving of 50/50 that equals 100%. Sometimes it will be 70/30, 60/40, 90/10, 99.5 to .5. And, sometimes it could even be 100% to the other person giving nothing. This point can be made by the mere fact that one spouse could suffer injury and become incapacitated thereby disallowing them to contribute at all. So it's quite conceivable that one could be the only person giving in a relationship. But regardless of who is giving more, someone needs to recognize that being still in marriage could be the turning point of the marriage or relationship and perhaps even save it. While this may not necessarily apply to all, some people – had they been *still* while in marriage – could possibly *still* be in that marriage.

The Art of Standing Still

When do flowers actually bloom? When do we actually grow and develop? These things happen during the dance of the night. Dancing in the stillness of the night is less about the timing of the dance and more about the timing of the stillness. This is because the timing of the stillness is to reflect on the dance that was done the moment prior. In music, a caesura is a pause or a break in the music. A pause in a musical piece breaks up the sound or movement. In this, it helps the listener to better appreciate the piece and/or anticipate what's next. Stillness is like a temporary stoppage to our motion. The stillness helps us to reflect on what happened prior to the pause, anticipate what is forthcoming in our lives, and know what we will need to arm ourselves with in order to withstand. Whether or not the motion is physical movement or even mental movement via thought, sometimes we have to pause and put people and situations on hold so we can breathe and move forward. So much action takes place at night. This action takes place not only in the atmosphere, but as well, in the spiritual-sphere.

We not only grow physically, but also spiritually, and are well on our way to our destiny. We do not take enough time to see the salvation of the Lord. If we did, we would also see that we possess so much power that we can command our destiny to come meet us where we are. Here is some declarative mindset manna for you: Don't be afraid to read this out loud.

When I am willing to be still, I am able to meet the challenges in my life head-on. When fear separates me from whose I am, with whom I am and with who I will become, then my faith will serve as a bridge to carry me over this Jordan. I will meet each new day with expectancy and an unyielding hope so strong that it will survive what should be catastrophic and serve the enemy notice to re-huddle and try again.

I am committed to being at my best even when things are at their worse. I am God's hands and feet on this earth, and with fortitude, I will walk with every God-given authority in my being – pulling down strongholds as I go. The God in me will affect those with whom I come in contact. I will cause change in the atmosphere wherever I go because of who I am.

I emphatically proclaim that no weapon that is produced with intent of ill-will against me will be of any success. While their weapons were designed to kill me, they only grazed me. It might wound my flesh, but my spirit deliberately advances and submits to the progress that my faith has generated.

Every attack was designed to make me weaker, but in my weakness, I have become even stronger. My new mindset of stillness tells me that the lesser I become, the greater Christ becomes in me.

So now, when it comes to the attack of my enemies, I can say, "Hit me with your best shot!" because my stillness determines my stance.

When we stand completely still in Christ, I believe we are better positioned to hear from the Lord. The Dance of night stillness says that we have an armor of light. So, if and when we are actually still and are in a moment of dance, the light will guide our steps. The dance of night stillness suggests that we should follow and not lead. During night stillness, it is usually dark, so why not allow the leader to lead? After all, He created the platform. He also inspired the dance, so allowing him to lead us is certainly in order. So forget dancing with the stars. Let's dance with the light…the light of the world.

Whether or not it is the two-step or whatever, during the dance of night stillness, we will do good to follow the leading of the master instructor. Our time of testing can take us to a stillness status that we never expected. It is then that we ought to dance as if our night depended on it. Only then can we appreciate the purpose of the light.

Manna Moment

Sometimes when we are mobile, our faith remains still. But often, when we are still, our faith can move us

That light serves as the conductor to all of the music…that is to say both the obstacles as well as opportunities that are present in our lives. When we learn to follow the light in our lives to a tee, then and only then will our passion and progress have been fulfilled, and the *movement* complete. Yes. Stillness can bring about enough discipline to put forth an order of completion in our lives.

There are people all around us who appear to have it all together – lock stock and barrel. They may appear to be well poised on the outside; yet there is so much unfinished business on the inside. There are some physically beautiful women – externally, who internally, don't like who they are. They are raw on the inside. There are well put together men on the outside who are full of insecurities and discontentment on the inside. We are only complete in Christ.

I have now been able to be still long enough to reevaluate some things in my life. The unfinished items must be completed;

and God has granted me the time to get them done. At this juncture, I refuse to live a life of regret. So, everything that God has ordered for me – and agreed to pay for, I will complete. As the saying goes, 'If God orders it, He will pay for it.' I however, had to be pretty much forced into stillness in order to begin the completion process where my unfinished business is concerned.

Manna Moment

The night blinds us, but the light guides us

If you stand completely still in Christ with your eyes closed, what you will find, is that the real true and present danger of night blindness, is your failure to see. Often, with our eyes closed, we see more than we would with our eyes open. Closing our eyes gives us more discipline to actually be still not only with our bodies, but also with our mind and spirit. Once we do this, it becomes much easier to stand in receipt of what God has to offer us: solace, peace of mind, fullness of joy, etc.,. Then we are able to – within the stillness – see the salvation of the Lord.

We have an armor of light that intrinsically glows in the dark. So, though we are blinded by the night, the internal light that we house, sees more than our physical eyes could ever see, and it guides us accordingly through a myriad of tests, trials, and necessary evils throughout our lifetime. Typically, light would be the thing that could serve to blind us…if we are looking directly into the light. However, maturity says that when we take on Christ, we become the light and after that, we lead others toward the light. How powerful is that – that we become the light we once sought after? In fact, the bible says in St. John, 12:32, *"And I, if I be lifted* up, will draw all men unto me." By the leading of the Lord, we become the conduit that serves as a translator for those who are in darkness to come into the light."

The pulse of your future rests on the stillness of your presence that is in the now of your tomorrow. So, dancing in the silent moments of your tests and trials will bring about thunderous applause from the heavens in the form of blessings that are and will be bestowed upon you.

DO YOU SEE WHAT I SEE?

Even without sight, one can still have vision. Think of it. There have been times when, even in my sleep, eyes closed and all, I have vision. I see myself in the future. I see myself completing projects. I see myself in the delivery room ready to give birth… ready to bring forth. I look better. I feel better. I not only see my destiny, but I'm in my destiny. Things are going fine. And then of course, I wake up. What happens with all of that stuff that's worked out while we are *still* at night? All of that insight and foresight? It is very important that we capture what we see at night while the night is still; so that in the morning, we can reconnect with our mobility, select the music, and dance. Both silence and stillness have incomparable rhythm. Stillness enables us to harness our potential while silence allows us to prepare for a powerful admission of promise.

Manna Moment

Once we graduate from the school of sight and are promoted to the school of vision, we will receive a private education that will cost us only our faith.

End of chapter questions and thoughts for discussion

1. Did you actually sing the doe re mi scale? Describe the feeling of holding on to the second to last note and not singing the final note.

2. Have you ever been in a relationship that ended but there were some things you needed to say – just so you could have closure? If you've been in a situation in which you never received closure, describe how you felt about the situation never having been closed. (example, unfulfilled promises from a parental figure that never materialized, friends and/or relatives who have passed on and there was an unresolved issue, etc.,)

3. Describe a period of growth from a time or experience where stillness yielded a great reward.

CHAPTER FOUR

SEEK AND GO HIDE

*T*his chapter was initially Hide and go Seek, but after carefully reading Psalms chapter 27, I decided it would be more appropriate that the chapter be Seek and go Hide.

Typically when we hide, we're often afraid of something, someone, or some entity. This chapter encourages us to hide – that is to say – rest – in Christ. And as we rest, God will shield us from the enemy who seeks to devour us.

Psalms 27 opens with *"The Lord is my light and my salvation; whom shall I fear? The LORD is the strength of my life; of whom shall I be afraid?"*

In order to recognize God as our light and our salvation, we would first have to seek Him. Are we that different from David that we can't repeat these words to affirm our decisive walk with Christ? As David, we too have enemies. But as long as God remains my light AND my salvation, there is nothing for me to fear. It's okay when I get weak because He is the strength of my existence and the very breath of my being. There is nothing on this earth that we need to be afraid of. Yet, fear will hold our faith captive until we command its release.

Psalms 27:4 says *"One thing have I desired of the Lord, that will I seek after; that I may dwell in the house of the Lord all the days of my life, to behold the beauty of the Lord, and to inquire in his temple."* How is it that one is able to hide as well as seek? What's the order? Do you hide first and then seek? Do you seek Him first and then go and hide? Or, do you seek while hiding? I believe that Psalms 27:5 suggests that we seek God while in hiding. Sometimes God puts us in hiding and in a place of solitude on purpose. A designated place of isolation where we are in our hiding place…whether it be in a pavilion, temple, house or tabernacle. Often what we seek is hidden in Christ, so we ought not seek after things that are not in Him.

How ironic is it that David connotes in this verse, that the single most important thing to him here is the thing that he will seek after. Hmmmm. This is almost the epitome of Seek and Go Hide in the sense that he seeks after that one thing that he desires, in order that he might dwell there…in the house of the Lord…forever…covered, sheltered, hidden. He chooses to follow after the Lord. This is so important to him, that it becomes his only desire. We know that it is his only desire, because after he seeks and finds God, he says that he want to behold His beauty; stay in the house of the Lord for the rest of his life; and he wants to inquire in God's temple. He wants to ask questions of God and continually seek Him. He wants to learn by asking of God. David recognizes that the power and wisdom of God is so exponentially infinite, that he could literally stay before God forever and still not be able to receive everything God has to offer.

Manna Moment

Our getaway can prove to be a gateway to stillness

Psalms 27: 5 *"He shall hide me in his pavilion. In the secret of His tabernacle shall He hide me; he shall set me up on a rock."*

Many of us perhaps have hidden *from* God; but have you ever been hidden *by* God? Some of us have been shielded physically, while others - spiritually. But in whichever way, God has a place for us…a getaway where we can go and hide in Him. It is a place like no other. It is a place of rest and release. Once we have rested in Him, we will soon after be prepared for a release. Talk about a release party! In this verse, God offers us cover in His pavilion. And, as if that weren't good enough, He offers an even more special and sacred place in the *secret* of His tabernacle where we can seek and go hide. It is a place of complete protection, solitude and oneness in Christ.

Once we have found ourselves to be hidden in Christ, we are heavily sought after. Now, we must begin to shed. This particular process of shedding comes about because once in Christ, we are charged with spiritual automatism where we begin the process of taking on the mind of Christ. How can we be in Christ and not at least love like Him? If any man be in Christ he cannot help but to change. II Corinthians 5:17 says, *"If any man be in Christ, his is a new creature. Old things are passed away and behold all things are become new.* The process of spiritual automatism says that I begin to take on His attributes so much so and to the point where the things that I do, are no more me, but Christ. (Galatians 2:20) *"I am crucified with Christ: nevertheless I live; yet not I, but Christ liveth in me: and the life which I now live in the flesh I live by the faith of the*

Son of God, who loved me, and gave himself for me."

THE PLACES WE COULD GO!

If we really take the time to look at this scripture verse, we will see that God has several places for his own to go:

Place – a concentration of population; Temple – a place reserved for prayer and sacrifice; House – shelter; dwelling place; Tabernacle – a portable dwelling place for the divine presence; Pavilion – structure connected to relaxation. Oh the many places we can go in Christ! All of these places provide us more than just shelter. They also offer us a hiding place, a place of peace and stillness; a place of re-giving, and receiving as well as a place of refueling, and a place of re-gifting;

REFUELING

As a place of re-fueling, it is impossible for us – carrying the weight of our circumstances – to enter into Christ and not fill up with His presence. If we are sincerely thirsty for God and want the fluidity of His everlasting love, God will fill our desires! It is necessary however, that the burden or weight that we carry in be left at the place where we carried it before we can refuel.

RE-GIFTING

As a place of re-gifting, it would be amazing to take an aerial view of the very many gifts we all possess. It is certainly nice to know that there is a place where we can go for re-gifting. In Christ, receiving the blessing of re-gifting never felt so good. If you have ever been the recipient of a re-gifting, you might have reacted sorely. This is where the giver may have repackaged an old gift previously given to them. Even if the gift was rarely used – if ever, the person receiving the gift, upon careful inspection of the actual gift, might be unappreciative of the gift. Perhaps it is because they perceive the gift to not have been carefully thought out, but a mere random giving.

Sometimes with children, you can give an old or previously given gift (especially a toy) a second time around, and it is as if the child had never seen the gift before. S/he will even react to the gift differently…but still appreciating the gift as well as the giver. Aside from the precious gift of the holyghost, there is an overabundance of gifts given to us all – in spite of our ability/ies. Therefore, in the spirit of re-gifting, sometimes God, the Giver of all gifts, has to meet us where we are, and re-gift to us some gifts that we have laid down at will. There are gifts that some of us have that we have lain dormant. Others of us have to receive the same gift in different packaging in order for us to acknowledge (and in some cases re-acknowledge) that the gift is ours and actually employ it. God's re-gifting reminds us that we should use the gifts that He gave us – to bless the Kingdom of God and empower others. God's way of re-gifting is sometimes repackaging and merely reminding us of the various gifts He had previously given to us in order that we unsurprisingly unwrap our gifts and employ or re-employ them.

CHAPTER FIVE

Mobile Mayhem

Manna Moment:

Mobility and agility are no match against stillness

We have to remember that our faith has a certain level of consistency. For one, our faith determines the feel of our situations; and our steadfast stick-to-itiveness. There are interwoven elements in our faith that gives texture to whom we are and who we become in Christ. There's an identifying quality to the character of the ones who use their faith. That texture, or quality, becomes us. Once we begin to use the very thing that builds us up, who we are far outweighs any mayhem that's happening in our lives. That texture or level of faith depends on where we are spiritually. The texture of our faith is contingent upon our maturation in Christ. If you are exercising that is to say, using your faith, then you're able to feel it. How do you feel faith? Well, if you use it enough, there will be a certain vibration…a sensationally rhapsodic movement…perhaps unheard, but strong enough to shift your system. Can you imagine? We embody faith that's strong enough to change the atmosphere…strong enough to topple strongholds at any intersection of life. I don't care how much mayhem is going on; stillness is a gift to believers. Read this comforting and well-known passage from the 23rd Psalms:

> 1. The LORD is my shepherd; I shall not want.
>
> 2. He maketh me to lie down in green pastures: he leadeth me beside the still waters.
>
> 3. He restoreth my soul: he leadeth me in the paths of righteousness for his name's sake.
>
> 4. Yea, though I walk through the valley of the shadow of death, I will fear no evil: for thou art with me; thy rod and thy staff they comfort me.
>
> 5. Thou preparest a table before me in the presence of mine enemies: thou anointest my head with oil; my cup runneth over.
>
> 6. Surely goodness and mercy shall follow me all the days of my life: and I will dwell in the house of the LORD forever.

I feel very comforted yet empowered when I read the first verse. The verse is empowering – yet relaxing. I feel invincible… as though I'm a little kid again, and I'm walking hand in hand with my father, who is about 10 feet and 5 inches and holds the record for being the tallest man in the world. And, that as I walk down the street, no one would even consider messing with me. The people who are staring, are not necessarily afraid of my father, but are rather impressed by his grandeur. Having Him with me is having any and everything I could ever imagine. And although I may not actually have those things in hand, I know they are in reach. And as long as I have my father always with me, I have access to the things I need...everything! Keeping him with me is like the state of being full to the utmost capacity. Even if I do want something, it's just that: a want. There isn't a need that isn't met. It's just one of the fringe benefits of me being with my father and my father being with me. I want absolutely nothing! I am satisfied. There is no need that is a challenge for my father.

No matter what is going on in life, we should remain calm. We have given our business over to our father to handle. In the second verse, He is my leader and my restorer. He just makes everything better. And, even though I walk in areas that are dark and threatening, I am so not afraid because I am not alone. If we could just know to keep God with us wherever we are, throughout our trials, we can survive because our shepherd, our father is with us and I'm immediately comforted. Even when it comes to my enemies. We have it backwards. We should not be fearful of them – just aware that they are there. Certainly, because my desire is to dwell in His house forever, if my will lines up with that, then goodness and mercy will both be with me for as long as I live.

Let's take a look at again at Psalms 23:2 *"He leadeth me beside the still waters."* Why *beside* the still waters? Why not *in front of* or *behind*? I believe this has much to do with comparison and alignment. Things that are beside each other can be easily compared. When we are led beside the still waters, we are parallel to it. Thus, it's easier to be compared. In the instance of the still waters, it's much easier to see just how mobile we are when we are beside something still. Even when we do finally settle down and become still, it takes a while for the mayhem in our lives to settle.

Have you ever been stuck in traffic? I have been running late to an appointment, rushed out and wham! I'm sitting in traffic frustrated and wondering why. Well, one day I was stuck in traffic on my way to work, and I happen to be able to look over the bridge and see the most beautiful body of water and thought "Wow. That is absolutely beautiful!" Another time I was stuck in traffic and actually appreciated it was when while sitting on the highway, I saw some of the most gorgeously landscaped flowers and thought "I wonder when they planted those…" The truth is… those things had been there all along… the flowers, the water and other things that go unnoticed when we are rushing about and are in mobile mayhem. Yes, there are times when we think we're stuck but often it's God keeping us stilled in order to keep us from an accident or an incident. So the next time your social commotion and locomotion comes to a halt, take the time to still your mind and look around you and see all of the things that you miss when you're moving. You will come to appreciate being still – even more.

End of chapter questions and thoughts for discussion

1. Can you think of a time when you were stuck in traffic, stalled in a long line at the store, etc., but that particular incident stilled and calmed you enough to remember or even create something for you (time to think, ministry opportunity)?

2. With so much hustle and bustle going on around us, mobility often produces mayhem. Please take some time to be still and celebrate those moments in time when you 'destinied' by accomplishing precisely what you set out to accomplish. In spite of the mobile mayhem, get still long enough to celebrate the goals that you've reached. Otherwise, you could spin your wheels trying to reach previously accomplished goals, or neglect to set new ones.

3. Has there been a time when you can actually remember the translation of one of your goals from thought to reality? Think of a life goal that you have set for yourself; and try to remember yourself meeting/completing the goal and/or becoming that thing that you set out to be. Write it down and discuss it.

4. Now think of something that you've always imagined you either would or could be, and then describe what you feel is keeping you from fulfilling that accomplishment.

CHAPTER SIX

THE BREAKING OF DAY

Manna Moment

An external occurrence does not constitute an internal uprising

Prior to the day breaking, as you sleep, the silence you experience can actually scream at you! Often, God ordains quietness as a medium by which to communicate with us. Sometimes we are overwhelmed once we awaken. And, though we are silent – still, the thoughts and ideas that are at the forefront of that moment in time when we wake, are dancing through our heads.

Something dramatic happens when day breaks. The word 'break' itself is an action word. The day opens up. At daybreak, the night is divided from the darkness and a new day is formed.

Stillness is like the shell on the outside of an egg. No matter how much you shake the egg, you can still feel the yoke moving about on the inside, but the shell remains still…that is until it is cracked or broken. How much more vulnerable are we when we are shaken, broken, tried and *considered* as Job in the bible? And can we still stand as a testament to regurgitate the triumphant 'Yet will I trust Him' declaration?

Many of us have been shaken but vow to remain still, hold fast, and stand firm. Likewise, many of us have been broken but yet remain still. God may not bless what you break, but He will always bless when you're 'broken'. Because our blessing point often takes place right at our breaking point, sometimes it's just about going through the process of breaking or being broken. When day breaks, we have new vision. Oh, what an opportunity! Lamentation 3:22/3 says, *"It is of the Lord's mercies that we are not consumed. His compassions fail not. They are new every morning."*

Stray bullets, fire, domestic violence – any number of things could happen to us during the time that we sleep – that could cause us to NOT see the breaking of day. Even suicidal *thoughts* could kill us. But, because of the Lord's mercies, and his unfailing compassion being and becoming new every morning, I am most grateful to be able to see the day break. We must learn how to capitalize on the opportunities that each new morning brings. When I am awakened with thoughts and ideas and don't follow through by immediately writing them down, often, the benefits are lost because the thoughts are forgotten. Seizing the day is so important. God wants so much, to break us out of our shell. Stillness does not mean complacency. One can be still and yet move into a whole new dimension of destiny. Complacency cannot move you, but brokenness will. Let's take a moment to compare complacency with brokenness…

- Complacency is designed to hold you in one position
- Brokenness is designed to move you.
- Complacency is a keeper
- Brokenness is a resuscitator

- Complacency breeds contentment but could produce resentment
- Brokenness sows seeds of humility
- Complacency serves to contain
- Brokenness maintains our level of grounded-ness; but prepares us for takeoff
- Complacency could deny us
- Brokenness can fortify us
- Complacency confines
- Brokenness liberates

Brokenness has the propensity to put a lean in your spirit and a lien on the property that is yourself, your soul – your all. Like silence, brokenness grabs and overtakes you as in a siege. When something is broken, it interrupts your moment of silence. Brokenness produces change – whether it is in mind, health, or spirit. God is the only one who can break the yoke on the inside of us, even destroy it, but manage to keep our outside completely intact. Brokenness distinctly disconnects us from the place where we are, and provides a direct shift into a new place. When we are shaken, the art of keeping it all together…is being unequivocally still. II Corinthians 4:8 tells us *"We are troubled on every side, yet not distressed. We are perplexed but not in despair. Persecuted, but not forsaken, Cast down, but not destroyed;"*

The awakening after a long night of rest is how I see the breaking of day. For some of us, going to sleep is the only way to be still. For others, sleep is the only way to secure our silence. It is no secret that some of us just talk way too much… so much so that we are unaware of the perpetual voice of God speaking to us at every turn; answering the very questions we ask of Him regarding our situations. Some of us have allowed answers to our questions to go into oblivion because we were not still enough to hear God's voice. God has to literally wait until we are fast asleep sometimes, just so that He can deal with us in our dreams. Some of us let our environment get the best of us.

We hold true to the saying, "You are a product of your environment.' Certainly, it is imperative that we have a relationship with God. Then and only then can we move forwardly. If we can't speak to our master regularly, how can we expect to speak to our mountains? We will have no effect when speaking to our situations. Our speak will be in vain when we cease to commune with our maker. If we don't eat, we will starve. When we don't wash, we will stink. If we don't put gas in our car, we will stall. When someone loves us unconditionally and gives us everything we need and we turn around and give our love and allegiance to someone or something else, we are ungrateful and we're cheaters. Imagine God withholding His blessings from us. Now imagine how withdrawn we would be if God were to withhold his *spirit* from us…

If you don't think that you have received a mighty move of God through experiencing a breakage, then you will. Don't worry. Just keep on living. Your breaking point is just around the *bend*.

Manna Moment

If we neglect to speak with our maker, we will lack the power to speak to our mountains!

End of the chapter questions and thoughts for discussion

1. Try to recall when you withstood a time of testing. Describe how it felt to have things seemingly topple before you but you stood still. Perhaps you or someone you know has or have had an ailment that was designed to take you or them out of here; but although the sickness was stirred up within, stillness was evident on the outside.

2. Describe a time when because you didn't stand still, your plans were messed up.

CHAPTER SEVEN

The Stillness that Moves Me

Manna Moment

It often takes tremendous energy to be still

Throughout our lives, we expend ourselves and forget sometimes that we have a place where we can go. I believe that true stillness has much motion. Stillness creates energy as well as synergy. Cradling yourself in the arms of the Lord will carry you through any situation. Being still in Christ is true stillness in motion.

When the sudden storms come in our lives, the peace of God has to resonate within us to produce the perfect storm. Our storms are designed for us. The perfect storm sets us up to be still – poised for promise and positioned for destiny. The perfect storm may do damage on the outside, but as long as we are still and go *'in'* during our storms, we are kept away from certain dangers. Going *'in'* allows us to watch from the safety of our home – or our hidden place. The perfect storm may uproot some trees that might have been standing for hundreds of years. The perfect storm could spiritually uproot and take away things that look good cosmetically, that you may prefer to hold on to; but in the end, we typically will recognize that those things were *meant* to be taken away from us. If you are not still, you may not be able to differentiate which sound means what. The perfect storm is tailored for us. It pulls us *in* and allows us to go *on*. The perfect storm landscapes our stillness.

For some of us traveling through certain storms, we just need to get to the rest area…the place where we can be still. Sometimes when we're traveling (driving) on a long road trip, we can be forced into stillness. We have to pull over to a rest stop and refuel, retool, relieve and/or replenish. So, you can see that there is a method to stillness. Being still is actually often essential to vitality. Stillness is preparation for impartation. Never operate so much in mobility that you either are unable to be still, or are unaware of your stillness. Stillness sharpens your discernment and brings about a keen awareness of God's presence. It allows us to be sensitive to every move of God. When everything around you is still, your mind is mobile. So when everything around you is in motion, be sure to have a specific place prepared for your time of stillness.

One is most observant when silent. It is a lot easier to inhale when one isn't speaking. Picture a cave and you in it. There's nothing but blackness all about the atmosphere. Let's use this as a time of reflection. Have you ever had an instance where it was almost yours - whose life was taken? How about a time where it should have been *your* car that was hit at the intersection but for whatever reason, you were at that point – intentionally stilled to be still…. and by now you've got a really good photographic reflection of mercy?

It should have been you who was let go from your job? It should've been you but you were shielded…that is to say – hidden…covered not just *by* but also *under* God's blood. Psalms 91 says, "*He that dwelleth in the secret place of the most high God, shall abide under the shadow of the almighty.* So, it's one thing to 'get' into the secret place, but it's a totally different thing to stay there and understand the purpose of the secret place. And, don't just stay there, but *still* there. To simply stop there might leave you idle and content with the status quo. But, to be stilled where you are leads you to desire completion where you seek to become whole. Your purpose will eventually be revealed while you are in the process (one of the toughest places to be). When we go to the gas station to get gas, showing up at the pump and pulling off without having filled up or gotten any gas at all, you have accomplished nothing. Either you will not get very far with the fuel that you currently have, or you may very well break down on the way to your next destination. How many times have we gone to the source and walked away empty because we refused to receive? This is what happens to some of us when we enter the house of the Lord. We waste time showing up as spectators rather than being participators. Why show up and not get what you need from the place where you need it? This doesn't even make good nonsense!

HERE'S LOOKIN' AT YOU

So many transitions take place before night actually turns into day. One of the challenges of being still – is because that being still is like the Christmas story – when a ghost of Christmas past, present and future meets you. It's like standing by and watching things happen in your life, and you are unable to do anything about it. Stillness is not driving but being driven. It is when you are being chauffeured and not even allowed to sit in the front seat. It's when you're in the back seat. A passenger seat would allow you to see too much and still be able to give directives like – "Watch out!" Don't hit that!" 'Slow down!' 'Speed up!'

Stillness allows you to be your own audience, double as an onlooker to yourself, your situation, all of your circumstances and see how you choose to handle your performance. So, here's looking at you: You looking at you, will allow you to encourage yourself to continue to fight the good fight of faith.

True stillness is when you *seem* to not be in control. But the truth about control is that control is exercising restraint. So stillness can be the ability to exercise restraint; but it takes effort to be still. There are situations that would cause for you to find your stillness, and hold it. Stillness can keep you out of danger. So turn control over to the master chauffeur, and just enjoy the ride.

The boomerang was designed to 'come back'. There is a difference between being still, keeping still, and standing still. Being still assumes that we have gone through a certain amount of testing; and we now have the ability to be. Enough things have taken place in our lives to the point where we can now take a step back from our current situation, be still, and evaluate exactly where we are. Keeping still is when you want to react, but refuse to. And, standing still is when you're given the opportunity to step in and make change but you don't, because you recognize that God will do a much better job than you. So you allow stillness to put you in a holding pattern, and you stand firm without flinching; You stand there when the winds blow and the rains come.

You stand there until God commands your peace to be still. Many times we don't realize why the winds blow while we are in our storm. The graciousness of God allows both the easterly and westerly winds to come from the opposite directions not to kill us, but to stabilize us. Allowing the winds to come from the two opposite directions actually keeps us standing. If it were only the winds coming from the west, it could surely knock us toward the east; and if it were only the winds coming at us from the east, it would likewise knock us flat on our faces in the direction of the west. But thanks be to God who allows simultaneous winds to come from opposite directions. This gives us balance. Since testing is necessary in order for us to prove our stance at stillness, then cement shoes are mandatory in order to stand firm in our storms.

Stillness is the emergent indulgence of motionless agreement with the night. Our ability to remain calm hinges – that is to say – rests on how we move into the season called still. Similarly, a great and mighty move of God rests on our ability to keep still. God in fashion cannot move until we are standing still. God is active, interactive and proactive. This season is similar to the season of wait. While we stand still, there's nothing else we can do except wait. While waiting doesn't necessarily call for us to be still, stillness definitely calls for us to wait. Can you serve while you are still? Absolutely. Servitude has to first come through our presence, character and attitude. Stillness prepares our heart and helps to produce an intentional availability.

There is strength in our still-ability.... which some may take for an inability to perform. But, perhaps God wants to take control of a situation. He does not have permission to do this when we are in control. We have to literally - turn things over to God – thereby allowing Him to be the executor of our will. When we allow this, God now has complete permission to take control. Why? Either we have not the capacity to handle our own business; or, we are dead. And, dying in Christ – has never been a bad thing. When God is in total and complete control of our business, finances, and life, we have made Him the executor of our will. An executor is one who executes, carries out or performs a duty or assignment. A secondary definition is a person named in a decedent's will to carry out the provisions of that will. So, what's the catch? You have to die in order for the will to live and be carried out! If not, then the will is invalid. We have to accept and recognize that true life begins by dying in Christ. So then as it says in Philippians 1:21, *"For me to live is Christ, and to die is gain."*

WILL YOU OR WON'T YOU?

If the best place to be is in His will, then for me, the worse place to be is in His won't. And, I for one dare not be found in the won't of God. It is so much easier just to be found in Him and in His will. Won't is an inoperative for God. While there are varying levels of God's will (perfect, submissive, permissive, etc.,), in the 'won't' of God is complete inactivity. Who has time to waste in the won't? Sometimes we think that by staying somewhere in the won't of God, we will somehow activate His permissive will. HUH??? If you're looking to make good use of your time, then I would that you not waste your time dilly-dallying in the won't of God. You will wish you hadn't. We should want to know what God's will is for us.

Manna Moment

Spiritual alignment gives us undeniable access to God's will

God's will is all over the bible. And, spiritual maturity takes you from a state of "can" into a state of "do". Can is the ability to do but it's when we put our "can" into God's ability that His Will is produced. Notice the scripture Philippians 4:13 "*I can do all things through Christ – which strengthens me.*" The can is affiliated with us. The will is God's affiliate. Your can is fortified in God's will. His will then becomes irrefutable.

When I first got saved – by way of receiving the gift of the holyghost, I was in the can of God. I believed that God could do anything. After all, He saved me! But after having been saved for a while, It's like your can automatically gets transferred over into the 'will' of God. My zealousness assured me that God could do anything. But then after a while, some storms came and the wind began to blow in my life. The tests got harder, and I still knew that the 'can' of God could. I just wasn't sure that in His will, He would.

A prophetic word was spoken – given by my young daughter. At about the age of nine, my sister asked Diamond what she learned in school this particular day. And, she replied that she learned about tenses. She said that she learned that the past is something that already happened; the present is happening, and anything that happens in the future has to have a will in front of it. The latter would be the prophetic.

Here's the translation: If you want it to happen in the future, you have to have a will. And certainly, if it's not just your will, but God's will, then it WILL happen. Of course, when your will is melded with God's will, then there aren't two wills but rather now - one. Because your will is inclusive of Christ's when you are in Him, He then comes into your will. You now have only one wish…one will. There should always be an "I Will" in your spirit. God is big enough to say "I am that I am." With His will favoring us, and when we are truly in His will, we are able to and should be bold enough to say: "I will what He is" and " I do what He wills" and " I will do what He says…." Then, when the wills become one, we ought to surely be big and bad enough to say the will, do the will, and become the will. Once two wills become one, the will then becomes a must! Becoming the will is the only thing that allows it to be performed in the future.

Manna Moment

Maturity takes you from a point of God's can to a place in God's will

But over a time, and a wealth of experience in standing still, I found out that God not only can, but God absolutely will. To have any situation come up in your life, you do BELIEVE that God *can*; but go through it, and you KNOW that God *will*! When your can becomes will and is lined up with God's will, it gives us undeniable access to blessings that are stored up for us. Please remember that the next time you are waiting on a blessing, the only thing between you and your blessings - is access. Here's a question we often ask … "Will God?" Here's something I heard Him say one day: "Will you?" The death of our choice brings to life – our will. Here's a declarative for you:

Vow of my life's will and Intent

I declare today, that I will turn over all of my situations, circumstances and struggles to God.

I will to die because I long to live…in Him. I declare that because the Lord is my shepherd, my will is not to want.

Since that my will is turned over to the Lord, mine eyes shall keep intense watch upon the hand of God; and I will rest passionately still and wait for Him to conduct and orchestrate my movement. With the total mastery of His hand, He shall wave me to rest. And I shall know that my every need is met and my heart's desires will have been granted; for I am complacent in Christ alone…dead unto life, and alive unto death…Now live I.

One of the hardest things for a believer to do is be still. I mean really! The request is that we give over our complete will to Christ, let Him do all of the work while we function as automatons. So what – you're the CEO of your own company? Give up your will and become an employee! It would still be your company; God would just own it. Isn't that wonderful? Because God owns it, I can say that it's mine. When we realize that God is the true owner of everything we have, we are in such a better place anyway. The air we breathe? Not ours… The house we live in? Nope. Not ours either. Now if we could just grab hold to the still truth that not even our life belongs to us, then it would be so much easier to die in Christ.

Death brings to life, the opportunity for some to receive. Death says to the executor of your will, that she or he then has to handle your business from now on. You have now given the executor the right to exercise his will as your own. When we allow God to become our will's executor, we transfer our will and right over to Him. Afterwards, everything He does, is done on our behalf; with our best interests at heart, and with His total control because we are now dead and have finally opted to give over to true stillness. We can truly fully and finally hand over our complete will to Christ. Being dead in Christ is merely the beginning of life for the believer. Where we mess up is when we turn our will over to God, but we don't sign or seal it. That's like putting a check in the mail to pay our rent or mortgage – but intentionally not signing it…trying to buy some time.

It's kind of like being in the back seat of your own car…unable to give direction to the driver. You know how we can be… bossy. Well, once we learn to be completely still in Christ, it's like handing over the keys to God and letting Him be the driving force for every aspect of our lives: Business, finances, relationships, need, and desire. Have you ever wondered why you've had so many ideas and they go absolutely nowhere? Perhaps you had the wrong person executing that particular will of yours.

I admit that it is hard to turn over total control to someone else. After all, you are the only one who knows exactly how you want it – right? Yes. But, our holy father in heaven is the only one who knows exactly how we need it. And He alone can build us up and firm our foundation. He is our carpenter. As often as we may say it, it is still seemingly so hard to let go and let God. But we are going to have to do this in order to bring forth in our own life's situations.

Not too many people appreciate the value of stillness. Because we always hear that time is money; so then, standing still seemingly does not monetarily bring forth. Spiritually speaking though, stillness brings about a value that is incomparable. In fact, when we really take the time to stand still, we can be sure that we will acknowledge thoughts and ideas that are worth their weight in wealth. When properly planned out, some of these thoughts can bring us untold wealth. Think of it. How many times have you had an idea go through your head, but you didn't act on it? You allowed it to be nothing more than a fleeting thought. This has happened to me countless times.

When McDonald's came out with the McGriddle, a very dear friend of mine – at the sight of the television commercial – exclaimed "Hey! That was MY idea!!!" I chuckled when she said it; but she was literally almost in tears trying to convince me that she is the one who came up with the idea! But with as many ideas as God have given me over the years, I realize/d that you do get a certain amount of time…actually, ample time to respond to the idea, and decide whether or not you will pursue it. And, if you don't, then someone else just may get that idea and have the wherewithal to work it through.

Now, if you're like me, you have gotten really great ideas and have not known how to make them work because you convince yourself that you don't have the funds to make it actually happen. And, there are more people in this world who had great ideas and no money; but strategically funded their ideas through sheer favor of God. It often seems as if the dark veil of that *other* math overshadows the ideas that I get. You know: not addition or subtraction, but *distraction*. The math that says it is impossible. The math that says it cannot be done…the math that takes you away from your focus and relocates your mindset. The math that multiplies your fears as it subtracts your faith and divides your trust – leaving you with only a fraction of the originally guaranteed promise that you had when you entered into the equation. Now, rather than an inflated vision, you're left with a deflated dream. Things such as doubt and fear – are detrimental to us. They keep us from our *expected* end. Doubts that keep you from believing you can attain and achieve; and fears keep you from even trying.

The math that we should apply ourselves to is the one we tend not to understand right away… the one that comes with all of the questions… "How am I going to pay for this? Who's going to fund my idea? I know this is a million dollar idea, but how do I make it work without money?" One word…FAVOR! Favor is frequently spoken of, but like faith, it is rarely cross-referenced, often underutilized and usually widely overlooked. During one seemingly excruciatingly long season in my life (did I say long?), favor and faith were my primary currency. Not even by choice, but by default.

Seemingly, when God wants us to consider something, He has to take us there. Even in our testing and trying times, God has to allow us to go through certain things. He literally has to take us there so that we can see that he has a hand in our deliverance. So, when we go through certain trials, we need to remember that one who has allowed certain things to happen in our lives is fully equipped to see us through to the other side of the trial. We are so accustomed to moving about; and we want to see God move by any means necessary. But a solid move of God will cost us some stillness. We sometimes miss the little things that God does for us for our failure to stand still. Have you ever heard the wind? How about God's still small voice? For an example, read I Kings 19:12 *"And after the earthquake a fire; but the Lord was not in the fire: and after the fire a still small voice."*

Keeping still truly allows you to see the goodness of the Lord. David says in Psalms 27: 13, *"I had fainted, unless I had believed to see the goodness of the LORD in the land of the living."* Abort movement and keep the still-ability within you. You can't afford to miss seeing God's goodness in your life. You can't afford to miss out on hearing God's voice. And as for the wind? The wind could literally carry your blessing from clear across the country directly to you. But you'll have to be still long enough to see, stand still to know it, and keep still to feel it.

Manna Moment

Sometimes a physical ailment brings about a spiritual connection

There has to be a keen tilt. You know the one where you actually incline your ear unto him, and hear him. I experienced a bout with vertigo some time ago. I didn't know what it was. I had to go to urgent care to get a diagnosis. All I know is that there was no balance. I couldn't stand up without immediately feeling dizzy. I had even fallen and felt more comfortable on the ground than I did - standing. Driving was difficult. The vertigo even impaired my vision so I had to pull over to regain some semblance of balance before moving on. Your whole life seems to be kicked off kilter. Because with vertigo everything is seemingly spinning, you are forced to be still. The only time I found some relief was when I was laying flat on my back. I used this experience as a lesson from God. I felt like God wanted me to *hear* Him so He had to make me still. There are things that we experience that we take to the medical doctor. However, some of these things are actually spiritual. We can't afford to lose our connection with Christ. He has need for us to hear Him when He speaks to us. But when we refuse, sometimes He uses other methods to get our attention.

We are often unmoved and unchanged by the things around us because we ourselves are typically moving. But once we can learn to be still, stillness itself will have delighted the heart of a mighty God to cause blessings to come our way.

Manna Moment

If you stand still, then God will move

End of chapter questions and thoughts for discussion

1. How still is your will?

2. Testing is necessary for survival. Take a moment to think of a test that you've gone through. Think of how you responded or reacted. How many times have we regretted the way we have responded to an event and wished we had responded differently? Jot down one of those experiences here either for personal reflection or to share.

CHAPTER EIGHT

A Season of Stillness

Manna Moment

While the seasons change continually, stillness will always stay the same

Stillness is a season that you can enter into by choice. I believe this is one of the toughest seasons in which to be. Some people are forced into this season by way of illness or loss. Others enter into stillness as a way out. Whether or not your stillness is mandatory or voluntary, for those of us who know Christ for who He is and are fully engaged with who we are in Him, we know stillness to be a way in.

Philippians 3:10 says *"That I may know him, and the power of his resurrection, and the fellowship of his sufferings, being made conformable unto his death;"*

There are so many who know God more now through their fellowship with him via suffering. Pain is a gift of intimacy that you might come to know Christ through fellowship. A season of stillness – whether forced or not - lends us the opportunity to commune with Christ as well as *hear* Him. Through sickness, this place of stillness is undoubtedly not a place of choice. The longer we are in sickness though, stillness allows us to sample the sufferings of God and relate to Him with a closeness that only the ironical warmth of suffering can bring. (II Timothy 2: 12) "*If we suffer, we shall also reign with him: if we deny him, he also will deny us*"

So many things can change for us in just a moment's time – without notice. In one of my instances of stillness, I cried because I was paralyzed with fear. I know though now, that some of my tests have promoted me. I recall being in a particular storm where I had to cry out "Lord, Don't you care?!" I know I am not alone in this. We have probably all had moments where we are in situations and wonder where God is, and how a God so great with all power, knowledge and sight, could look on and allow some of our situations to happen to us or our loved-ones. I know that God heard *and* answered my cry. Even at the time of this writing, I have not as yet experienced a resolve to a particular situation, but I know that God answered my cry as I clearly heard him say "I will make restitution." I believe that some of us are blessed through and by the prayers of our parents and *their* parents. Some prayers that we plant, we may think go unanswered. They don't. Sometimes our seed are the recipients of some of our prayers. They simply were predestined to inherit the harvest. There are seasons of planting, seasons of watering, and seasons of increase.

In a prayer one night, I thanked God for increase; and in this, I was not thanking God for an increase in finances or fortune and fame. Rather, I cried as I ended the prayer because when I said increase, what I actually saw in my mind's eye was a heightened level of testing…and increase in a series of faith teasers. I saw things to come that would immensely try my faith. But beyond that, was the increase of my faith. If we aren't challenged with crises and through various tests, then our faith does not have the opportunity or the *privilege* to increase. I have learned not to ask 'What else could go wrong?" In my experience, it is an open door for a test to greet you at that door. However, we need to have tests in order to balance out our levels of faith.

God didn't make an example *of* himself *for* himself. He did it for those who would come after Him. He did it for us. Our parent's parents lived and sacrificed for our parents. Our parents took certain stands and stances so that we might experience a better walk. Likewise, we live for those who will come after us.

Manna Moment

A season of stillness is a treasured time of connectedness to Christ

A season of stillness begets a life of stillness. The time is more valued in retrospect…after having left the season of still. I might have been stuck in my season if I hadn't learned the art of standing still. Even through my fears, my season of stillness eventually produced a motion of faith. In spite of a series of testing, a season of stillness and a lifetime of challenges, my still-ability remains intact. While certain tests bring about a mandatory stillness, I have reached a point of maturity where I now get still by choice. Stillness on a voluntary basis has not only changed the way I see things, it has also changed the way that I approach various situations.

Without a doubt, stillness moves God. Often it says that we are tired of running around in circles and are ready for God to take over. This move of stillness on our part is seemingly voluntary to us, but is mandatory - that is to say necessary - in order for God to fully operate on our behalf.

Can we be partially still and see a move of God? Sure. But seeing a move of God and experiencing a move of God are two totally different things. If we want to experience a total move of God, then we are going to have to be completely still in order for permission to be granted from us to God. This permission says that we have taken our hands out of the mix and want/need God's help. Thank Him – still; love Him still; appreciate Him still; And no matter what you do, in all of your stillness, still-stay in Him.

Manna Moment

Being still at a time of war creates a piece of confusion for the enemy

End of chapter questions and thoughts for discussion

1. Describe the season that you are in presently.

2. Discuss how an act of stillness could help you through this season.

CHAPTER NINE

STILLNESS ON DEMAND

Manna Moment

When we allow it, true Stillness conceals us at the same time that it consoles us

There are many different genres of picture taking. One of those genres is still life photography. By definition, it is the depiction of inanimate subject matter, most typically a small grouping of objects that are either manmade or "natural." One example is an arranged bowl of fruit or a bouquet of flowers. Word is that still life photography is a demanding art. Still life photography, more so than other types of photography, such as landscape or portraiture, gives the photographer more leeway in the arrangement of design elements within a particular composition.

THE STILL LIFE

Still life photography is an art. One in which the photographers are expected to be able to form their work with a refined sense of lighting, coupled with compositional skills. The still life photographer makes pictures rather than takes them. Knowing where to look for propping and surfaces also is a required skill. (Wikipedia) Wow! Now imagine that we are living the still life – where we are the subject matter...and the photoghapher places us in a particular grouping or arrange us however s/he chooses. We give the photographer enough leeway to arrange us by design – within the composition of our lifetime. And, our master photographer has all of the compositional skills needed to be our author and photo finisher. (Hebrews 12:2) *"Looking unto Jesus the author and finisher of our faith; who for the joy that was set before him endured the cross, despising the shame, and is set down at the right hand of the throne of God."*

There are times when God - desiring us to be still – will allow things to come our way that will demand our stillness. In terms of our 'propping and surfaces', our God knows what to use to 'prop us up'. However, there are times in our lives when we have fallen and cannot seem to get up. This is when God (our photographer) has to physically pick us up and place us on a surface that is soft enough to provide comfort and healing; and yet strong enough to protect and hold us in place until we heal. Our tests are aligned to create the canvas upon which our lives rest; and give us the backdrop that will give onlookers a sense of timing to the picture. There's a saying that 'A picture is worth a thousand words...' The surfaces that the photographer selects are skillfully chosen. For those times when we think we can't make it, we may have to be propped up on an even surface in order for us to rest, and regain some semblance of stillness.

Still photography is important in the life of the believer. Still photography captures where you were at the particular time of your stillness. It also helps to pivot and route (or re-route as it were) us to a place and set time of manifestation in our lives. I am intrigued by the fact that lighting is so important to the photographer and how the picture comes out. As oppose to motion picture, when still photography catches us, our image is made permanent on light-sensitive materials. So, to those who are practicing stillness, our light is what holds us in place and gives validity to our appearance. In still photography, lighting is everything. In the life of the believer, our light - the light that emanates from within us is everything. While living the still life is extremely hard and takes much discipline, the still life leads to the good life, and the good life (with total preparation) will lead to eternal life.

In addition, the chronology of our stillness brings us to a set time of manifestation – which brings about change in our lives. So, when it comes to standing still, we must be properly positioned - with the right amount of lighting for the camera; and the intentional lack of action. Because where stillness catches us, is where the snapshot will keep us. So, hold still in the position that you expect to be blessed. Still photography in the life of the believer allows us to return later, and view the picture that captured us in the season where we were. Now we can have a flashback praise. Picture that... knowing where you now are, you get the picture of where you were; and you can praise on your way to where you will be – allowing your internal light to shine through your external life, and generate enough power to lead you to the eternal light – which will guide you to everlasting life.

End of chapter questions and thoughts for discussion

1. Think of and give an example of a time when you were forced to be still but later realized that even though you weren't still by choice, it ended up being for your good.

2. Write a statement that conveys how you got from your then to your now – describing any period of 'still' in your life.

Manna Moment

An abundance of stillness leads to a life of more defined mobility

CHAPTER TEN

AT THE CENTER OF YOUR STILLNESS

Manna Moment:

The Power of our Stillness is centered in Christ and the Center of our Stillness is the Power of Christ.

Have you ever heard the saying "Find your center"? This is often said when things are topside turvey – inside out. Well, your 'center' is a still place that allows you to focus and recalculate your direction. It's a point of transmittal…a place where all things mobile can be tranquilized. Sometimes when we are silent with our mouths, we equate that to stillness when in fact, it isn't necessarily so. We can keep our mouth silent and still speak equally as loud with our facial expressions, body language and actions. Therefore, unless our mind, body and soul are all still, then we fall short in the fullness category of stillness.

At the center of your stillness is the tree in Psalms 1:3. *"And he shall be like a tree planted by the rivers of the water, that bringeth forth His fruit in His season; His leaf also shall not wither and whatsoever He doeth shall prosper…"*

Stillness is like being planted like that tree. Some people are placed, and some are planted. There's a strong difference between the two. Something that's placed is a temporary. It can slide, be moved - not just by someone physically shoving or removing them from a place, but when you're in the beginning stages of stillness, even a stare, a glare, a look could be enough to shift you. Something "placed" can easily be "displaced". But when we have learned to be completely still in Christ, we understand that something planted is much harder to move because it has already taken root....it has that VINE-connection! Our vine connection happens because we are 'in Christ'. It takes a lot of work to uproot something that has been planted.

The enemy uses plans. But, when something is planned, it is not as effective as a "plant". Plans are designed to be changed, moved, altered, omitted, done away with...even forgotten. But a plant is steadfast. A plant takes root, and thus is not easily moved. A plant's branches can be clipped, but that only allows for more growth...new growth. Tests and trials come to "clip" you to prepare you to receive more. New growth happens through maturity. We often talk about going through our various levels of testing. But especially when we are talking about being like the tree in Psalms chapter one, I believe that one of the most important things to remember about our tests is not that we merely go through, but that we learn through our testing and GROW through. That growth will always take us to the necessary level of maturation. Total stillness requires a mind transformation. (Romans 12:2)

Furthermore, we are unable to bear fruit unless we stay in Christ. When you look at stillness, new growth is like going from just being planted as a seed, to growing into the tree you are to become. And, pruning is necessary for us to bring forth the right fruit in the right season.

Some branches, while they are still attached to the plant as a whole, are yellow, and will soon be cut away, or often fall off on their own. Some hold on, and blend in, thinking that the naked eye can't see that its color has changed, and it has no strength of its own. Sometimes the deadened branch doesn't realize that it can no longer act as a chameleon, and that its colors no longer change. So while they think they can still be in Rome and do as the Romans do, they don't realize that the Romans know that they are actually intruders - sticking out like a sore thumb. God always has us right where he wants us. We must continue to be *"steadfast, unmovable, always abounding in the work of the Lord..."* (I Corinthians 15:58) Our labor is not in vain...rather it is in vine. The work that we do is stored up in the vine.

When we are "grounded" we realize that our strength is in our roots. Sometimes it is hard to be "instant" out of season, but we must continue to be instant in season as well as out of season. It is easy to grow in season, but even out of season, with our roots connected to the vine, we can continue to grow and prosper through the vine connection. Furthermore, the attackers don't usually venture out to the pavilion where the vine is...it's in the secret place. It's in the secret of his tabernacle where he hides us. And God will set you upon a rock. God is the only one I know who can set you upon a rock, and you can grow there and take root. Anything else needs dirt, and water. We need God; and God needs our stillness.

Manna Moment

Stillness powers your progress

Being still will allow you to do far more than you would otherwise be able to do mobile. That is the power of stillness. Stillness in Christ makes us stronger in Him. I am stronger because I have endured a season of involuntary stillness. During this season, my stillness encased me and showed me as dead to the enemy. But, because I was still, I was merely resting in Christ.

WEIGHT LOSS

Hebrews 12:1 *"Wherefore seeing we also are compassed about with so great a cloud of witnesses, let us lay aside every weight, and the sin which doth so easily beset us, and let us run with patience the race that is set before us"*

Stillness has served as protection for me. I was engulfed by storms that were weathered by my still-ability. Were I not still, I never would have made it through some of my trials. A season of stillness is what made this book come forth. I lost my job, some of my dignity, and along with that, my will to continue to fight sometimes. I can honestly admit that even depression set in because I couldn't with my natural sight – see my way out. But I held on long enough to still my way out and allow my faith to see where I was going. It soon became evident to me that all of my loss (outgoing) was necessary in preparation for my gain (incoming). Sometimes things have to either be put away or taken away in order for us to experience a true replenishing. I consider myself to have been gainfully unemployed because every lesson learned has been a valuable one for me. I have been able to watch God take me to different levels of faith in Him. I have allowed Him to be my provider and caretaker. I have allowed Him to literally be my everything in this season. And just as He promised, He has come through for me every single time. What an advantage! While I'm not particularly fond of living on the edge – waiting to see *how* my need would be met, God has proven His reliability to me over and over again.

Recognizing Jesus Christ as your center – helps to focus a little beyond the point of stillness and into the point of rest. Wow. Now this is solace at its best. It's totally safe to say that death is a point of total stillness! How is it then – that we as children of God – can avoid dying in Him? It's simple. We can avoid it because our wonderful savior is such a gracious gentleman, who gives us choice. Often when the choice is to live or die, overwhelmingly, we choose life. Well, those with a right relationship with God know that the only true way to live is to die. After all, had not Christ died for us, we would not otherwise live.

Our life is through and in Him – only. Death is the vehicle through which life is wrought. I find that Christians – more so than non-Christians fear the things we don't understand. When on the contrary, we Christians should be the ones who 'get it'. Often, people who Christians consider 'nonbelievers' live as vicariously as possible because they better understand Hebrews 9:27. *"And as it is appointed unto men once to die, but after this the judgment:"*

Not knowing when we will breathe our final breath, we as people of God should want more than anything to live our fullest life – in Christ with the understanding that death is not the end, but merely the beginning of the believers' life in an eternal life with Christ.

God wants so much to get back in our center. With so many distractions, circumstances, and everyday life issues, from the time that we receive the gift of the holyghost – when God was the center of our joy – until now, retrospectively, take a look at where you are now in your relationship with God; and recall where you use to be. I believe in all of us, we can attest to a time when nothing else mattered…nothing else but God. And, with God in the center, He has the opportunity to direct all of the traffic in our lives. So when Christ is at the center, in your center, and is become your center, then everything else that takes place around you, you can handle because of the fact that you removed yourself from the center.

FRONT AND CENTER

When we allow God to take center stage in our lives, then He will in turn receive all of the attention. Because we are in Him, and He receives us unto himself, then He will get the praise and all of the well-deserved glory. There's something to remember about center stage. As the one in the center receives the attention, this self-same center will likewise receive the deficit. But what we typically seem to want to do, is take the center in order to receive the blessings and the glory; and we tend to want to throw God back in the center when it's time to receive punishment, chastisement and trials. Actually, we have it all backwards. We should be willing to endure the pain and put God in the center to receive the glory. God is more than willing to help us through all of the trials in our lives but we must put Him back in the center.

There is a specific story in the bible where God was center stage…when the crowd cried "Crucify Him!" We can't get much more center – than the crucifixion of Christ. Christ was at the very center of the cross. And, while at the center of the cross, we were absorbed in Him and in the center of His thoughts. As Jesus withstood each nail; as He was bludgeoned and His flesh beaten beyond the point of recognition, His stripes took center stage. Every whelp, bruise, cut was center…centered on your and my freedom.

We have to get back to the point where everything we do is centered in, on and around Christ. Our lives will be to a certain degree, free from a large amount of stress. For instance, if I know without doubt, that God is going handle everything, why should I have to stay up for the entire night trying to think of ways to make my situation better? When we place Christ back in each of our individual centers, then when troubles come, we can just hand things over to Christ and it's a done deal.

Our being in the center puts us in a better position to *a*sk, *s*eek and *k*nock (Matthew 7:7). While it was Jesus who was crucified on the cross, you should still be able to close your eyes and take a good look directly at the center. If you focus on the center long enough, then you ought to be able to see that the shadowed and protected image just beyond Christ, behind a randomly crimsoned cross… branded but approved…is (_____) you. Can you see yourself? Perhaps you don't recognize that it's you. Sometimes we forget that our sin-stained, guilt-ridden selves – have been generously concealed by the cross and not given over to man for misinterpretation or misrepresentation; and that Christ's love and attraction for us has placed us in *His* center…His heart.

AT THE END OF THE DAY

The sound of stillness rings in like a ton of falling bricks suddenly having received wings; and then rather than falling to the ground, they simply float in the air as if feather-light. Likewise, when we apply the enduring intensity of stillness to our circumstances and our lives, it will allow us to take weightless stances that will give way to weighted victories. Even if but for a moment, the art of stillness allows us to soar into flight, where we are relaxing, resting and progressing in Christ, then we are well on our way to finding our peace in the puzzle of this life. Even the most heightened level of stillness produces fluidity. God came that we might have life and that more abundantly (John 10:10). Thus, stillness is strategic and serves to ultimately change us – the way we process.

Therefore, once we are centered and stilled, we can expect to be accelerated into our destiny through a mighty move of God on our behalf.

When we still ourselves intentionally, we are far from stuck. Even involuntary stillness positions us to eventually walk away better and stronger than we were before – physically, spiritually, mentally and emotionally. The enemy would have you to feel as though you are stuck. However, stuck is a place where mobility is not an option. Moreover, if the enemy can get you to the place where you *think* you're stuck, then you will live in a position of controlled complacency for as long as he can keep you there.

The continuity of our stillness is stabilized by the unending flow of the love of God. When we are truly standing still, God and only God is qualified to transport us to a newer and greater dimension of and in destiny…with revelation that takes us from faith to faith, glory to glory and from our still activity into active stillness where we will achieve an overwhelming interaction with peace. *"And the peace of God, which passeth all understanding, shall keep your hearts and minds through Christ Jesus"* (Phil. 4:7). It is very easy to find it hard to be still…and could be quite hard to find it easy to be still. Nevertheless, still is as still does. Thus, stillness is doable. Your stillness will shift the climate and cause others to take note. To find oneself in stillness is to find the peace of God. A period of still will undoubtedly transport you from an old *place* into a new *position*.

Ironically, even the atmosphere *remains* still while the night *turns* into day.

·····················

Manna Moment

When we get to the place where we can feel
motion through our stillness in Christ,
then we will have reached the place where we can yet find
Christ in motion at the center of our stillness

Manna Quotes

All quotes are the original and should not be reprinted without written permission of the author – Pattie Walden.

Standing still serves as an internal mobilizer; as keeping still serves as your stabilizer

A voluntary yield toward stillness could lead to a mandatory move of God

While Movement is counter-productive to stillness, stillness will often provoke movement

Standing still gives us a great view of the future!

In the darkness is where our level of faith is revealed

One can live without sight, but die without vision

Remember that faith is the vehicle through which sight is produced

Our faith is not powered by sight, but our vision is empowered by our faith

Negativity deactivates our faith

What we say with our mouths affect the direction of our feet

How well we see in the darkness could determine how well we walk in the light

Sight shows your temperament. Vision reveals your testimony

Sight shows what your situation looks like in the natural. Vision reveals a very triumphant 'you' in the spiritual

Sight allows you to be all that you can see. Vision allows you to see all that you can be

Vision gives sight the permission to see what God has in store for your future

Stillness is a platform for performance

Stillness often reveals a movement of faith

In stillness, our strength is not compromised. On the contrary, it is maximized

Sometimes when we are mobile, our faith remains still. But often, when we are still, our faith can move us

The night blinds us, but the light guides us

Once we graduate from the school of sight and are promoted to the school of vision, we will receive a private education that will cost us only our faith

Our getaway can prove to be a gateway to stillness

Mobility and agility are no match against stillness

An external occurrence does not constitute an internal uprising

If we neglect to speak with our maker, we will lack the power to speak to our mountains!

It often takes tremendous energy to be still

Spiritual alignment gives us undeniable access to God's will

Maturity takes you from a point of God's can to a place in God's will

Sometimes a physical ailment brings about a spiritual connection

If you stand still, then God will move

While the seasons change continually, stillness will always stay the same

A season of stillness is a treasured time of connectedness to Christ.

Being still at a time of war creates a piece of confusion for the enemy

When we allow it, true Stillness conceals us at the same time that it consoles us

An abundance of stillness leads to a life of more defined mobility

The Power of our Stillness is centered in Christ; The Center of our Stillness is the Power of Christ.

Stillness powers your progress

When we get to the place where we can feel motion through our stillness in Christ, then we will have reached the place where we can yet find Christ in motion at the center of our stillness

Author's Biography

PATRICIA WALDEN

Pattie is a dramatist, playwright, songwriter and more importantly, a change agent. She has a passion for the youth, a love for music and a desire to see people encouraged. While serving as a coach and mentor for youth, Pattie's ministry has translated into her being a motivational speaker and an inspiring thought-leader and serve as a life consultant to church and community leaders.

A professional announcer, national voice-over talent for radio and television commercials, Pattie is dubbed as one of the most versatile voice artists in the U.S. Her voice is heard by millions of people throughout the country and abroad to AOL users everywhere saying: "Welcome! You've got Mail!" for AOL's 9.0 optimized and personalized version. This accomplishment was recounted on the front page of The Daily Press newspaper in Norfolk, Virginia. Pattie is a member of the American Federation of Television and Radio Artists (AFTRA) union. In her spare time, Pattie doubles as the Christian comedienne , the dear "Mother J" – performing at church conferences, as an opening act for concerts, plays, private functions and at community and school events.

Pattie received her formal education from Franklin Pierce University in Rindge, New Hampshire. She has a bachelor's degree in Mass Communications with a minor in Theatre. Raised in Hartford, Connecticut, she is a native of Jamaica, West Indies. Pattie currently resides in Atlanta, Georgia; and is the proud mother of two children: daughter, Diamond and son - Levi.

Regardless of the assignment, Pattie functions as a visionary and catalyst. A teacher at heart, her gift from God is her voice. Whether heard on television, radio, through her character "Mother J", through song, spoken word or through her writings, Pattie intends to minister to the masses with her God-given voice for whatever venue He allows. She is on assignment to continue to write ministry pieces that uplift, inspire and affect change.